NIRVANA IN A CUP

The Founding of Oregon Chai®

*The True-Life Mother-Daughter entrepreneurial
journey that brought an ancient tea out of the
Himalayas and through mom's kitchen to brew up
the $75 million-dollar business, Oregon Chai.*

THE ULTIMATE AMERICAN DREAM!

by
Tedde McMillen, Co-Founder
with Heather Hale

MOBY
Press

Copyright © 2006 by Tedde McMillen

Published by MOBY Press
Portland, Oregon

Printed in the United States of America

Library of Congress Control Number: 2006927621

ISBN 0-9786475-0-5
9780978647506

To: Sawyer and Hailey

ACKNOWLEDGEMENTS

First, I would like to thank my daughter, Heather Howitt. Without her this book and the amazing experience I had at Oregon Chai, Inc. would not have been possible. My husband, David, put up with a sticky floor, people running in and out of our house at all hours, cases of Oregon Chai stacked in the hallway and basement, and never flinched when it came time to pay the phone bill or have a lien placed on our house. To my son, Sean, who helped convince one of our first customers to try Oregon Chai in their restaurant and for his inspiration for a pattern for our packaging. My sister-in-law Carol McMillen, and sister Merre Friend who loaned us some start-up cash and read and edited this manuscript for me; David Friend who quelled my concerns as this book approached deadline and sister Gerre Vickers, nephews Eric, Adam and Coby Vickers who stepped in to clean up our messes when necessary. Thanks to Heather's husband, David Howitt, who supported and encouraged us and to Uncle Jack Fulks who told everyone who would listen in Spokane, Washington, about Oregon Chai.

Thanks to my partners: Heather Howitt, Lori Woolfrey, Carla Powell and Brian Ross. We were a great team. Each brought unique talents that complemented and balanced the group, along with the ability to work independently, not always an asset. Very special thanks go to George Spencer, Lori's Dad and our attorney. He was always available to listen to our concerns and full of good advice. Thanks to our advisory board: David Barrish, Dwight Sinclair, Joel Lewis, Rex Bird and the late Mike Wigell, who took a chance with no immediate compensation but with huge hearts and the willingness to share their expertise with enthusiastic, struggling novices. And to our wonderful, dedicated, PATIENT employees who all had a sense of humor: Jonathan Howitt, Kurt Peterson, Marla Barrett, Jill Raefield, Carey Johnston and those who came later who continued to grow the company.

Thanks to our first customers: Al Volo, Broadway Bakery, Umbra Penumbra, B.R, and Nature's Fresh Northwest who were willing to try a new, unknown product and, of course, to those customers who continued to support the Oregon Chai brand.

Special thanks to all of our investors but especially to Bruce Pomper who took a huge risk and invested in a brand-new, untried, company, with inexperienced principals and an unknown product. To Crown Point: for helping with direct placements.

Thanks to Devan Shah for not only teaching me about tea, but for providing the start-up Oregon Chai with a presence in his booth at the New York Fancy Food Show. To advisors Janet Busch, Dan Eischen, and Tom Jones, who taught me about food processing on a much larger scale than I ever thought possible. Thanks to the staff of the Oregon State University Food Science Department and the Oregon Department of Agriculture for providing information and answering questions. Also Allan Bennett at the F.D.A. for his patience and help explaining the intricacies of working with the F.D.A. and labeling requirements. The Small Business Administration for approving our loan and Dave Cutter, bank manager, who was willing to take a risk and gave us the much needed cash. Thanks to Harry Pattison for his incredibly creative, humorous copy and the staff at Prideaux, Sullivan, Pattison, and Clevenger for their award winning packaging and Jordie Welles, Creative Director at Lewis & Partners for conceiving the brilliant tagline, "Nirvana, Now Available by the Cup"™.

A special thanks to my writing instructor at Portland Community College, Nyla Booth, who encouraged me to publish this book and to my editors, Jodi Giddings who corrected my grammar and made my "be" verbs active and, of course, Heather Hale who added warmth and humor. And, finally, thanks to my graphic designer and webmaster, Dennis Foster.

Table of Contents

DESSERTS

SNACKS

Introduction

Why an introduction? Why not just read the book?

I must admit that I am one of those people who never bother to read introductions or forwards. I guess I'm just too impatient. I want to get right into the meat, to taste the succulent innards like Tom Jones, with juice running from the corners of his mouth. I lust after the story and want to ravage the prose.

However, since YOU have taken the time to read this introduction, I thought I'd use it as an opportunity to THANK YOU for buying and reading this book. I sincerely want it to be worth your efforts.

My editor told me an introduction is written to tell you, the reader, why I felt compelled to write this book. That is as good as any place to start.

During my tenure at Oregon Chai I was always being asked to speak at luncheons and various business functions. I was happy to share our story. In fact, I wanted to - I appreciated the opportunity. Not only to share our pride of our great company and raise awareness of our terrific Oregon Chai product - and hopefully sell even more of it - but I truly wanted to inspire and empower others toying with the idea of taking that first entrepreneurial step, those with a little recipe in their pocket that was dying to be shared.

People would often ask me: "How did you do it?" I often heard other women say (sorry I never heard a guy say this - it always seemed to be women who would say): "I'd love to start my own company, but I just don't have the money." Whoa, where's the passion? Where's the drive? Where's your spirit? You don't have to start big - in fact, it is much better if you don't. It is so much easier to work out the kinks when you are small, as you will see in this book. It's called the learning curve.

So, my goal in sharing our amazing journey was to not only record my experiences founding Oregon Chai but to give you that little nudge to help you to overcome your fears and gather your courage to - as Nike says: "Just do it!" They had to start somewhere, too - and I bet it didn't start with a million bucks!

I also hope you are able to chuckle at our many mishaps. Shake your head and say to yourself: "My God, it's amazing they made it." You might even think we were successful in spite of ourselves. I'm sure more than one of our consultants thought so, but where would these successful businessmen be if we hadn't crawled through the mire, gotten our fingernails filled with muck and brought this little cup of tea to a roiling boil that could stand shoulder to shoulder with the big guys: Lipton, Nestea, and Starbucks? Yes, ma'am, we had passion. We had drive. We had a great team. We had a wonderful product and perfect timing.

To this day, I remain amazed at how groundbreaking events transpired and essential people appeared at just the right moments: doors opened just as we needed them and phones rang offering viable, much-needed solutions. I sometimes wondered whether it was karma, some great cosmic power, or just plain, old-fashioned, good luck.

Oh, yeah, things went wrong but we picked ourselves up, wiped off the sweet, sticky, slurry - and started all over again.

So pick up this book, have a good read, enjoy yourself, and if you have an entrepreneurial spirit, I hope it will inspire you to follow your dreams.

NIRVANA
IN A CUP

The Founding of Oregon Chai®

SECTION I:

The Harvest

C H A P T E R   1

Karma

"**M**om, call the embassy! I've been arrested!" my twenty-year-old daughter, Heather, pleaded from halfway around the world. It was three o'clock in the morning. On Christmas Eve.

Heather had been teaching English as a Second Language in Nanjing, China, about a thousand miles from Beijing. This was just weeks before the Tiananmen Square tragedy - before any of us had any idea that racial tensions were about to explode - or that my daughter was on the tipping point of this intensifying storm.

"There's been some trouble between the Chinese and African students," she breathlessly explained, "They need help."

"What happened?" I asked, feeling helpless in Portland, Oregon.

Gauging the fear in her voice, I sensed instinctively that it was very important that I remain composed. For both of us. But I was terrified.

"There was a riot in the African students' dorm," she exclaimed. "The Africans wanted to get out, to escape to Beijing, to get home to Africa. So they marched together to the train station (it was safer for them to stay together as a group). They just wanted to get home. But the Chinese wouldn't let them. They were surrounded and couldn't get out. They were throwing bricks and rocks at them."

"Whoa, wait a minute. Who's throwing rocks?" I asked, still waking.

"The Chinese students, teachers and people from the village, nearly ten thousand of them surrounded the train station. There were about two hundred African students inside along with six Americans. The Chinese soldiers wouldn't let any of them leave. They were holding them as prisoners, to question them. The soldiers wanted to figure out who incited the riot."

"Everyone was frightened," she continued. "There was no food or water, so I took some in - and they arrested all of us. The soldiers picked me up and dragged me onto a bus. I was kicking and screaming. I lost my fanny pack with my passport. We've been on a bus for hours. The soldiers brought us here. They said it was for our own protection. I'm the only one they allowed to make a phone call."

"Hold on, where are you, now?" I asked.

"I don't know where we are. We drove all night," Heather answered nervously. She shifted into a whisper: "Mom...there are seven Chinese soldiers with rifles all around me. You have got to call the Zambian Embassy and tell them what's happening. You are the only one who knows --"

The phone went dead.

A mother's nightmare.

My husband, David, groggily asked what was happening. I shouted something unintelligible and grabbed my bathrobe. He blinked, uncomprehendingly and rolled over. I let him sleep. There wasn't anything he could do right now. I wasn't sure there was anything I could even do. Morning would be soon enough to worry him about our daughter.

I called 411, plowed through the phone book and searched desperately for a phone number for a Zambian Embassy in Portland. Or in Seattle. Or San Francisco. But it was hopeless.

No one answered any of my calls. It was 3 AM. On a holiday.

But it wasn't like I could just go back to sleep and deal with it in a couple of days, after Christmas.

I tried Portland's local newspaper, The Oregonian. They gave me a number for a hotline to the State Department in Washington, D.C. I called and raced through what little I knew.

"We'll try to find out what's happening and get back to you, Mrs. McMillen," an agent promised.

Over the next few days, they called frequently, updating us, filling us in, assuring us that Heather was safe. It eased our anxieties - barely.

Finally, after three long days - and with zero explanation - Heather was released from the prison compound and unceremoniously exiled from China.

Her passport was returned with a firm: "You are no longer welcome here."

She had been held longer than any of the African students.

Heather had planned to teach in China until her work visa expired the following spring. But even though she had a life there - a job and friends - she was forced to pick up and leave - on the spot.

Ever the trooper, Heather decided to make the best of her situation. She headed for India to try to end her trip on an up note. She had no idea that this little side trip would change the rest of her life.

On the way to India, high in the Himalayas, Heather lodged at a camp for the Indo-Chinese border patrol. Blonde and blue-eyed, she had always felt out of place in Asia. Added to the fact that she tended to explore off-the-beaten path rural destinations, she often wondered if the locals had ever set eyes on a foreigner. While hardly statuesque by American standards, at five feet, four inches, Heather was noticeably taller than most of the natives she encountered. Not to mention, it was rare to see any woman alone and independent in Asia - especially in the eighties.

She and a friend decided to hike one of the remote trails used by the patrolmen. As they strode through the mist, a small, wooden lean-to appeared. An elderly man who easily looked like he could be a centenarian, stood before them. Hungry and thirsty from having hiked all day, she and her hiking pal eyed the dozen hardboiled eggs atop the simple, timber bench. Alongside, were tiny little ceramic cups filled with a sweet, spicy, milky tea he called "chai."

Heather tried a cup and loved it instantly. Then she had another. Then another. Before she knew it, she had downed thirteen cups. She was hooked.

Chai became Heather's staple as she traveled throughout India. She delighted in finding it on street corners and in every restaurant and hotel - it was everywhere she visited. She relished it in its endless variations.

Each region used different indigenous ingredients. Every family recipe had its secret. No two cups of this ubiquitous delight were ever the same.

Heather studied the chayvalas (the Indian word for people who make or sell chai). Some simply tossed cardamom and a handful of tea pellets to boil in a pan of sacred cow or buffalo milk. Others used a symphony of exotic, fresh spices. But they all added sugar, making unique - but always pleasingly sweet - teas. Heather fell in love with chai.

When she returned to the states, I finally got to ask her: "What incited the riot?"

I'd been dying to discover more the entire time she was trekking through the Himalayan Mountains.

"There was a lot of racism in China," Heather explained. "They called the Africans "Black Devils." The local community and the Chinese students were jealous because they felt the Chinese government treated the African students better than they treated the Chinese students. The African students were all on scholarships and had better housing. They each had private dorm rooms while the Chinese were squeezed in eight to a room. The Chinese students were used to these conditions but they felt the Africans were being spoiled. They knew that the Africans were very poor, and came from underprivileged countries, but they felt the racial favoritism was unfair."

"Not to mention, they were from completely different cultures," Heather continued. "The Chinese only date after they've known someone for a long time. And only after both parties are sure they've got serious, long-term intentions whereas it's no big deal for an African to ask a complete stranger out on a casual date. So, obviously, when African men asked Chinese women out, it caused a lot of misunderstandings."

"Plus, the African students came from a much more laid back culture," she concluded. "They hung out and listened to Reggae and smoked pot while the Chinese were really studious and serious. The Chinese thought the Africans were being disrespectful. They thought the Africans were lazy and took everything for granted."

"Did you ever figure out where they held you?" I asked.

"We were jailed just outside of Nanjing in a large hotel room with rows and rows of beds. They woke me up at three a.m. and led me into an empty, white room," she recalled "where twenty Chinese men wearing blue suits interrogated me. They wanted to figure out who started the riot."

I had been following the incident in the newspapers and had read every article I could find on the riot and its aftermath.

"The San Francisco Chronicle said the Chinese soldiers insisted that you pay for your room and board during your imprisonment," I told her.

"Can you believe their nerve?" she asked rhetorically.

"It claims you shouted 'No!' That sounded like you," I said, laughing.

"I was pissed," she continued, "They wanted me to cover their expenses while they held me against my will? I thought: 'How can they do this to me? I'm an American!'"

She hadn't been frightened, only angry. This was the Heather I knew. Ever strong. Ever courageous.

Heather returned to school at UC Santa Cruz where she rented a room in a house at the base of the university hill. Each morning, she'd bicycle the two-plus miles uphill to class. She was thrilled to discover chai being served at some local restaurants and espresso bars. The two coffee shops on campus sold fresh chai to masses of weary students.

Every morning, Heather would bike to the closest espresso stand. If they were sold out of chai, she'd pedal a mile in the opposite direction to the entire other side of campus and pay as much as three dollars a cup to get her daily fix. She was a case study incarnate of the coffee house culture about to explode on our cultural horizon.

Upon completing her degree in anthropology, Heather left Santa Cruz. She visited friends in Boulder, Colorado, where she happily discovered her favorite drink served at many of the local espresso bars. But after returning to Portland and making an extensive search of every coffee bar she could find, she was astonished to discover that no one in her home town offered chai.

So, Heather started to brew it herself.

C H A P T E R 2

A Sweet Spicy Tea

"What is it?" I asked.

"Just try it," Heather replied eagerly.

I sipped. "It's unusual. Sweet. With lots of interesting flavors. Kind of exotic." I said.

I swished the warm, rich drink around in my mouth. I tried associating the flavor with something familiar, but couldn't come up with anything quite like it.

"I don't know," I said, "It's different...I'm not sure if I like it."

"I make it all the time," Heather boasted. "All my friends love it."

I wanted to know more: What was it? Where did she find it? How did she make it?

"It's chai," she explained. "A spicy tea. Chai is the word for tea in lots of languages: Hindi, Farsi, Russian, Persian, even Swahili. It's prepared differently in each region. They add mint in Egypt."

"I discovered it in India," she continued. "It's also called masala chai. In Northern India, they boil milk with black tea and spices then add a lot of sugar making it sickeningly sweet. But if you order chai in Southern India, you just get black tea. Chai hit the U.S. in the sixties, where it was first served at ashrams and communes."

"What's an ashram?" I asked.

"Oh, Mom, you know, it's like a hippy commune, sort of like a Hindu monastery. Gandhi stayed in an ashram during the struggle for India's independence. They were big in the sixties."

"Well, I'm happy with my chamomile. Or plain black tea. Though I do like warm Ovaltine before bed - but I doubt this could ever replace any of those. But it's interesting," I said, thinking that would be the end of it.

When Heather first introduced me to chai, I was forty-eight years old and had just been laid off. I had been the Manager of Admissions where I hired, trained and supervised over two hundred ushers and gate attendants for the local entertainment venues. But my prolonged job search had become tiresome and I had grown weary of the mounting resume rejections.

Since I had married young, I had never gotten my college degree. The goal of finishing my college education before my fiftieth birthday became a new, defining goal. So, in September of '93, I enrolled full-time at Portland State University.

Heather and I got to be students at the same time. She had just completed her undergraduate degree in anthropology and was also enrolled at Portland State University in an Urban Studies master's program with an emphasis on recycling. It just seemed as though she spent all of her time weighing garbage. Heather and I both enjoyed our flexible student schedules.

Heather continued making and serving her home brewed chai, always trying to convince me how great it was. One day, she said, "You know, Mom, I think we could sell this stuff."

"If you're serious," I said, "I'd be happy to help you."

Pleased, Heather looked at me slyly and said: "I want to call it Oregon Chai."

"How'd you come up with that?" I asked, surprised she'd already considered this.

"Well, Oregon is known for its espresso-related culture. I think having Oregon as part of the name will give it a positive, cutting edge, health-oriented spin."

Naming a product is an important step. To succeed, you need a product name that can be branded distinctively without any negative connotations. Oregon Chai was simple. Straight to the point. It was important to me to honor her instincts, her vision. After all, the whole thing was her idea.

To refine the recipe, Heather plopped herself in the middle of the cookbook aisle at Powell's Bookstore in Portland, one of the largest booksellers in the world. She surveyed all the Indian cookbooks and was surprised how few chai recipes she could find - especially given how rampant the tea was in its home country.

Comparing potential ingredients and possible brewing strategies, she began to create her own signature formula. She was adamant that it include her favorite flavor: vanilla. It had to be smooth and delicious, rich and indulgent. She wanted to find that delicate balance between a chai that would honor its Indian heritage yet appeal to the modern American palate. Heather's goal was to get people to love chai just as much as she did.

After extensive research and tons of tasting and testing, Heather was finally satisfied. It wasn't long before even I came around and was enjoying a cup of chai as much as my Ovaltine. Even my husband and Heather's father, David, convinced throughout the process that he would never be weaned from black coffee, realized one day that he'd completely abandoned his morning coffee and, almost by osmosis, now shared his daughter's addiction.

"If you can convert me," he finally conceded, "you can convert anyone."

I had just about everything we needed to make chai already in my cupboard at home. Heather's childhood bedroom got transformed into our home office, stocked with office supplies from previous (failed) ventures. Rent and overhead weren't issues we even worried about. Our phone bills and utilities would just somehow be absorbed into our regular household expenses, covered by David's self-employed architectural income. The question of start-up capital just never occurred to either of us (which was probably just as well since neither of us had any - save about three thousand dollars each - on deposit from student loans).

Once Heather arrived at the basic recipe, we had to scale it up to make much larger batches. Having read all about the disasters that can occur as recipes are doubled, then tripled, then increased ten-fold, I was wary.

But we were lucky. Each batch of chai just worked, regardless of the scale we brewed.

Next, I began to look for ingredient suppliers. Teabags were available in bulk for just ten cents each from Safeway. Nature's Fresh Northwest, a natural food store nearby, offered spices in bulk.

We learned a couple of tests were needed to determine how to best process and package our new food product, most importantly: one for water activity and another to test the pH level.

My Associates of Arts degree in music had hardly prepared me for food science. I hadn't a clue how to even begin to test for these things but I found a food lab near our home. I took them a sample of our proposed chai and asked them to perform the necessary tests.

We registered with the state of Oregon that we were doing business as "Oregon Chai." I called the various state departments to find out what regulations we had to adhere to and what licenses were required. The Agriculture Department sent me reams of information on building requirements, warehousing and sanitation. I realized immediately that we couldn't just make chai out of my home kitchen: we had a dog and a cat. So much for our "cottage industry." We had to upgrade to a commercial kitchen even before our first batch.

I knew that many of our area churches had kitchens so I phoned the church nearest our home, The Sunset Hills Church, and asked if they might let us rent their kitchen for a day or two a week. Amazingly, they agreed. And without checking a single reference or insisting that we sign a waiver, they handed us the keys to their building for just two hundred dollars a month. Off my very first phone call, I solved the problem. This isn't going to be so hard, I thought.

I next learned that before we could start manufacturing and selling chai, we would have to get the church's kitchen approved by the Oregon

Department of Agriculture but their inspectors were so backlogged, we had to wait weeks before anyone could visit our site - and we couldn't begin production until they signed off on our rented facilities. When the big day finally arrived, our inspector called and cancelled.

"I'm so sorry," he apologized. "There's been a power outage in a fish processing plant and assessing that health risk is a more urgent priority."

"I understand," I said, disappointed, though I certainly understood and concurred. "When can we re-schedule?"

"I know you've been waiting a long time for us to get out there. I promise you, your inspection is next. It's at the top of my list."

Later that week, as I was shopping in my local grocery store, I grabbed some fresh fish that was on sale and placed it in my cart. It suddenly dawned on me: what if this is the fish from that lot? I put the fish back on display and opted for chicken instead. Just in case.

Finally, the inspector arrived, examined - and approved our kitchen. We were licensed. He told us that we were greenlit to begin operations but that it would be a good idea for us to get liability insurance.

I didn't believe our chai would make anyone ill, but providing a product for human consumption is never without its problems. Besides, given the fish plant incident, I thought we should get some protection just in case we encountered any unforeseen challenges. After some research, I learned that every distributor we might potentially work with was likely going to require it, too, so it would behoove us on all fronts to get liability insurance from the get-go.

Not having a clue where to begin, I phoned the broker for my homeowner's insurance. His company didn't handle that type of coverage but he referred me to a professional acquaintance who did. Ultimately, we bought a policy that covered our first year. Future premiums would then be calculated off our annual sales. That seemed fair enough. Who could predict what our sales would be one year from now?

I visited a branch of U.S. Bank and introduced myself to its manager: I'd better establish a good relationship right from the start, I thought. We set up our first business checking account and were approved for a corporate credit card. I was euphoric. A corporate account, I thought, just like the big guys. The VISA card gave us a five thousand dollar credit limit - a tiny bit of precious liquidity.

For over thirty years, my husband and I had shared just one car. For the first time, we would need separate transportation. A friend of my husband's owned a local Ford dealership, so I called him and explained to him what I thought I would need: a car to haul equipment, supplies and ingredients to the church and return home with batches of brewed chai for deliveries. I picked out a new Ford Escort wagon that would be perfect. This was the first vehicle I'd owned solely since before my marriage. The new car was undeniably a prudent business purchase, to be sure, but it was a proud moment and milestone for me in launching our new business - and my enhanced independence.

While waiting for my new car, I chatted with a salesman who was originally from India. I told him all about Oregon Chai.

"You think your chai is good," he said with a clipped Indian accent. "Wait 'til you try Kashmiri chai."

I was intrigued. I'd never even heard of Kashmiri chai.

"Please, tell me more," I said.

"I know nothing of its ingredients," he said. "But my grandmother used to make it and I just loved it."

I made a mental note to research that variation. Right now all I could think about was getting this little start-up off the ground but if it really did work then this may be information I could use. LATER!

CHAPTER 3

Try Chai

Heather and I took samples of our product to a few potential customers for their feedback. Broadway Bakery, just across the street from Portland State University, where we were both students, was one of our first visits. I loved to splurge on their tasty scones - the best I'd ever had in Portland.

The owner was a large, friendly man who reminded me of Santa Claus - you just wanted to hug him. I mentioned our project to him several times, but he was a busy man and rarely had time to chat.

Finally, he relented: "Okay, I'll meet with you."

Elated, we arrived at the bakery after the lunch rush had subsided. A handful of stragglers lingered at small tables scattered about the converted Victorian home. He led us upstairs to the seating area in the garret where sunshine poured through beautiful windows. We sat down at a light-drenched table.

I'd brought our chai, blended with milk, in a quart-sized mayonnaise jar. I could hardly contain my excitement as I handed him a cup and watched as he sipped.

"I like it," he said. "I'd be willing to give it a try."

"Great!" I said.

He asked how he would serve it, heat it and keep it hot.

"I don't want to have to go through some elaborate mixing process," he insisted. "Serving the chai must be quick and easy. We're a very busy shop and I'm only interested in items that can improve my business."

Heather interjected, "There's a company in Santa Cruz that makes chai fresh every morning. They keep it in a glass coffee maker over a low heat. When someone orders a cup, the barista mixes the warm concentrate with hot, steamed milk, just like a cappuccino."

We talked about getting a small, electric percolator to keep the concentrate warm. This sounded like a reasonable idea to all of us. We agreed that a sweetened, spicy tea concentrate - minus the dairy component - was the best way to take our product to market.

"Without the milk," I said, thinking out loud, "the chai would be much easier to package - not to mention, much safer to store. And the consumer could choose their dairy base of choice - soy, non-fat or whole milk - whatever - upon ordering. That would open up the marketplace dramatically."

"Well, continue refining the process," he said. "If you find a simple solution, I'd certainly be willing to give it a try."

I found a small, one-quart percolator that was the perfect size for a crowded counter or an espresso cart - but it offered no controls. When turned on, it would heat the product but would not maintain a low simmer and I was afraid the chai would burn. So perhaps that wouldn't work after all.

The solution we came up with was to keep the concentrate at room temperature (or refrigerated after opened). The barista would add the consumer's dairy preference and then steam the whole mixture together.

I went back to the lab and had them test the concentrate. It turned out, Oregon Chai concentrate was just about as safe as a food product could be. The pH was low which meant it was acidic - and that's a good thing, I learned, because most microbes do not grow in highly acidic products. As long as it was handled using sound food safety practices, Oregon Chai was safe for human consumption and fairly easy to package. We had our answer.

Next, we needed a label for our new product. Since our chai was selling only in espresso bars for food service, our product's nutritional information didn't have to be broken down for the public, so we decided against elaborate labels, saving us precious capital.

Heather had a natural eye for color and design - as well as a professional architect for a father. So, using the shape of the state of Oregon along with a font she created herself, Heather designed our first label. She drew the template and printed the copy by hand.

I took Heather's original drawing to a local print shop and copied it eight to a page for a master, then copied these onto Avery label sheets. In the evenings, I trimmed each little state-shaped label carefully with scissors. Taking five to ten minutes to cut each one, it was a tedious and time-consuming process.

When we were finally ready to make our first big batch, I filled my car with supplies: four pots with lids, spices, teabags, a few bottles of honey, measuring spoons and cups, funnels, filters, pitchers, dozens of plastic bottles and lids, labels and boxes - and drove to the church.

The kitchen was located in a Sunday school classroom in the church's basement. I hand-carried everything by myself - about eight, oversized, cardboard boxes - down two flights of stairs and through a long, narrow hallway. It took several trips to get everything from my car and into the kitchen.

An electric stove with four burners and a mammoth sink were at one side of the large classroom. The rest of the room was packed with several bulky, round tables and lots of chairs.

The stove had two large burners and two small burners so I measured water into two three-gallon pans for the large burners at the back of the stove and two one-gallon pans to fit on the small burners in the front. As the water heated, I minced the ginger and measured the spices, then plopped the entire mixture into the boiling water.

As the brew steeped, I washed all of the bottles and caps. All bottles were made of number-two plastic. Heather insisted that we use recyclable materials whenever possible. I agreed, our company wasn't going to mess up our planet. If anything, we were hoping to make life a little bit better, one sip at a time. Once the tea had finished steeping, I added the honey. I held my face above the pots and inhaled, my head spun in the blissful aroma. I tasted the concentrate and then mixed it with whole milk. I sipped the sweet, warm drink - and loved it. Chai was really growing on me now that we had nailed the right recipe. This is so good, it should please anybody, I thought.

I happily filled each bottle, twisted on the lids and wiped them clean and dry. I removed the backs of the Oregon-state-shaped labels, adhered them to the front and placed the warm, full bottles in neat little rows in cardboard boxes.

After I finished, I washed the dishes, scoured the stove, counters, tables and floor and packed everything back into the boxes and made the eight trips lugging everything back down the long hall, back up the two flights of stairs and outside to my car.

In four hours, I had brewed eight gallons of Oregon Chai. I wasn't concerned about my hourly rate - I was too busy and quite honestly, I was really enjoying the process.

I delivered our new concentrate to Broadway Bakery and he agreed to buy our first quart for $1.50. I was elated. Until I realized on the drive home how ridiculous that price was: not only did it barely cover our hard costs, but it didn't allow any margin for sales, marketing or distribution - much less profit.

I hated having to go back to my first client and tell him that the price we quoted him yesterday would have to be raised. He was amazingly understanding. He "got it." After all, he was a businessperson, too.

Outside Heather's neighborhood grocery store in Lake Oswego, where she and her fiancé, David Howitt, lived while he pursued his law degree at Northwestern, was one of her favorite espresso carts. Heather patronized this retailer almost weekly. Chatting with them frequently about her passion for chai, they soon became a loyal customer - and arguably one of our greatest fans. They were forever pitching our chai to all their patrons, handing out free samples. They even posted a letter-sized sign that read: "Try Chai" on the front of their cart. We thought this was a great advertising slogan because it helped people to pronounce Chai (it rhymes with "try").

We had undeniably come up with a new and outstanding drink - an instant hit. Now the challenge was getting the word out there.

I would usually brew chai in the mornings in the church's kitchen, drive home, put away my supplies, change my clothes and make espresso bar deliveries. Because of all we had learned about pH levels and food storage (specifically that our chai would be safe stored at room temperature), I kept any extra chai stored in our basement.

Marketing and sales are constant challenges for every business, from startups to the Fortune 500, but we had to create consumer awareness from scratch for an entirely new and foreign product before we could even begin to secure market share of a category that didn't even really exist yet. All with no budget.

How were we to whet the appetite of customers who had no idea how hungry they were for a taste of Nirvana? Since the majority of our customers had never even heard of chai, we realized that to woo new customers, we were going to have to pound the pavement - literally hand a cup of fresh chai directly to people on the street and make them "try chai" on the spot. It turned out to be a very rewarding and successful approach.

"What is it?" they'd ask.

"A sweet, spicy tea latte," we'd answer.

"Oh, but I don't like tea," many would say.

It was always amusing to watch their reaction. Their skeptical eyes would transform instantly. They'd raise their eyebrows as they peered into the warm, steaming cup, inhaling its rich aroma. A smile would creep across their faces as they sipped the smooth, sweet brew.

"Oh, that's so good!" they'd often say - usually with great surprise.

One customer told me: "it tastes like Christmas." Once we were successful in persuading them to try chai, they would usually buy some - and most were hooked from then on. The product sold itself. We just needed to get people to try it.

We'd prospect local coffee houses between our classes at Portland State.

I was excited to get my second major appointment. One owner told me, "Come back around ten o'clock tomorrow." I was thrilled. Game on.

The next morning, I brewed some fresh chai and poured it into a thermal pitcher so it would be steaming hot and ready for him to taste. I changed my clothes, jumped into my car and drove downtown. As I walked into the shop, I realized the chai had leaked out of the pitcher and had dripped all over the front of my slacks. I was embarrassed, but what could I do at this point? I used the counter to hide the mess on my pants and introduced myself to the clerk and asked for the owner.

"He's busy right now," the clerk said. "May I help you?"

"No, thank you. I'll just wait until he's free," I said.

The café was crowded with customers eagerly awaiting their morning jolt of caffeine. The owner overheard our conversation and approached.

"I'm very busy," he said, "I don't like sales people just dropping in without an appointment."

"But I- I have an appointment," I tried to explain. "When I was here yesterday, you told me to come back this morning -"

"-- I don't know who you are," he said, visibly upset, obviously having completely forgotten our conversation.

I left immediately, deflated and humiliated, too embarrassed to defend myself further.

My son, Sean, introduced our Oregon Chai to a small, late-night coffee bar - and they loved it. Now we had three steady customers. This business just might work, I told myself.

A week later, Heather and I visited Nature's Fresh Northwest, a popular, local natural food store known by many residents as "Nature's." Heather followed-up with their food service director and managed to secure an appointment at their corporate offices with the chief buyer. This was a huge breakthrough for us.

The buyer directed us to sit in their conference room. Intimidated, Heather and I sat next to one another on the same side of a twenty-foot-long conference table. He sat at the end. We slid an embarrassingly-unprofessional mayonnaise jar filled with homemade chai into the middle of the table.

I sat there thinking to myself: why didn't we put a label on this? Why didn't we at least put it in the packaging we're using for the espresso carts? Wincing, I was pained at the realization of how over our heads we were. There were just so many things you think of after the fact. Thank God our product could stand on its own in spite of our inexperience.

We told him about our chai, how Heather had discovered it in India and began our presentation. The buyer was kind and spoke freely with us but the entire time he listened wearily, rubbing his temples with his fingertips.

"You know," he interrupted, "less than fifteen percent of the products I see ever make it to the shelf."

Heather and I glanced anxiously at one another. Neither of us knew what to say. An uncomfortable stillness shrouded the room.

Miraculously, a voice from outside the conference room broke the awkward silence: "Heather? What are you doing here? Is this your chai? Can I taste it?"

Heather turned around and recognized one of her friends, luckily, one of Nature's employees, standing at the conference room door.

"Sure!" Heather said, grateful for the diversion.

Her friend entered and tasted our chai. She recruited all of her co-workers to join her in the room and told them all about Heather and her chai: a blessed, unsolicited third-party endorsement right in front of her boss.

By now, a large group of people milled about the conference room, tasting and talking about Oregon Chai. The buyer had long since disappeared in the crowd. I was pleased when I finally spotted him, reclining in his chair with a whimsical look on his face, watching the excitement buzz about the room.

"How much do you think our customers would pay for it?" he asked from the back of the melee, to nobody in particular.

"A dollar ninety-nine," one employee offered.

I couldn't believe my ears! I thought that was excessive.

"What size container would they expect?" the buyer asked.

"Sixteen ounces is about right," someone answered.

I made a mental note: a dollar ninety-nine, sixteen ounces. Wow. That's pricey, but at least we'd be covering all the expenses I had forgotten to calculate on our first sale to Broadway Bakery.

When the unlabeled mayonnaise jar was empty and all the chai was gone, the employees returned to work. We thanked the now bemused buyer, picked up our empty jar and drove home, grinning the whole way.

A few days later, we received a call from Nature's.

"We want Oregon Chai at all four stores in our espresso bars," the representative said.

I phoned Heather immediately and said: "We just got our first order from Nature's!"

Bring to a Boil

That summer Heather and her good friend, Lori Spencer (now Woolfrey), went hiking in the old-growth forest near Opal Creek. Heather and Lori had been high school classmates and college roommates. They were old friends. Lori held a degree in art from Dominican College in San Rafael, California and knew a lot about color and design.

During their hike, Heather told Lori about our endeavor and Lori had some great ideas about how we could market our chai.

"Would you be interested in working with us?" Heather asked.

"I'd love it!" Lori said. "When can we start?"

And thus, our third partner entered the picture.

More and more people were trying - and liking - Oregon Chai. Heather, Lori and I served all our friends and family members chai. In fact, we encouraged everyone we knew to give it a try.

I took our chai to a family picnic on the fourth of July. We did consistent quality control wherever it was sold. Luckily, for our strapped budgets, the espresso bars serving our chai usually doled out free samples, so we could do random taste tests without going broke.

As the demand increased, so did the pressure on me to keep up with production. More awareness and interest meant brewing more tea to fill the orders, which meant producing an increasing number of stickers and cutting more of those dastardly little state-shaped labels. It seemed endless. I felt like I was constantly trimming. My fingers were blistered from the scissors, which made peeling off the label backs painful, nearly impossible. At five to ten minutes each, it was a ludicrous process.

"I need real labels," I finally laid down the law. "Designed and printed. I can't keep doing this. This is ridiculous."

Heather agreed we had to find a way. I couldn't wait.

In the interim, sales continued to increase and it wasn't long before we received another exciting call from Nature's.

"Would you be interested in selling your product in our retail outlets?" they asked.

"Absolutely!" Heather said.

We were ecstatic. But if we sold our chai retail, not only would we absolutely need better labels but that suddenly opened up the door to a whole new host of regulations concerning providing consumers with very specific nutritional information. Now we had no choice but to come up with new labels. It's funny how sometimes your needs overlap and force you to do what you need to do anyway.

We were entering a whole new arena. Entering the retail side, we'd be marketing directly to the consumer. But growth is good, right?

I phoned the U.S. Food and Drug Administration trying to figure out what the new retail label requirements would be. They faxed me reams of literature that afternoon. So much that I thought the fax machine would never stop. Whenever I needed assistance, the F.D.A. provided help immediately. They turned out to be an invaluable resource - a refreshing change for a governmental bureaucracy.

Still, it was a daunting challenge to wade through all that red tape and jump through all those legislative hoops to figure out exactly what information had to be detailed on the label. Listing our ingredients in order of quantity (biggest proportion to smallest) was one of the requirements. Using a particular font and type size was another. But this was all just the tip of the iceberg.

F.D.A. regulations required that the nutrition and ingredient statements reside on a particular panel of the container with the copy a specific distance from the top or bottom of the panel. We also included instructions on how to prepare the chai latte by mixing the concentrate with milk.

We took our chai back to our local food lab and had them analyze it to give us the correct nutritional information to publish. I asked the F.D.A. inspector if they would proof our label before we had it printed en masse to make certain it met all their requirements.

"I'm sorry, we're not allowed to do that," the inspector said.

"Then how will we know if it's right?" I asked.

"You will be notified if it's not," he said.

Great! I thought. If it isn't right, then who pays for the new labels? Us, I'm sure.

I shared my newfound knowledge with Heather who made an appointment with a graphic designer. Over one productive weekend, Lori and Heather met with the designer and came up with new labels, business cards, table tents (small signs that sit on a table advertising a product), and a poster.

The table tents, posters and business cards were printed on recycled paper using vegetable-based inks. The poster described Heather's discovery of chai in the Himalayas. Our logo was changed from the shape of the state of Oregon to a small teacup with an illustration of Mount Hood, Oregon's largest mountain and Heather's favorite ski destination seemingly steeping, or rising like steam out of the cup. We were pleased with the results.

Then Heather told me the price.

"It's going to be twenty-five hundred dollars," she said. ·

I was flabbergasted. Floored. This was the first time I had ever encountered design costs.

"That sounds excessive," I said. "We have to do something less expensive."

"This is not expensive, Mom," Heather explained. "Besides, it's already done."

"What!?"

After I collected myself from the shock of her committing to that major of an expense without even bothering to clear it with me first, I suggested snidely that since she was the one with the extravagant tastes and that projecting an expensive image was important to her but not to me, then maybe she should pay the bill.

"I don't have any money," my daughter confessed.

I sifted shock from disbelief.

"I invested everything I had in some 'hot stock' (her boyfriend) David recommended to increase my capital," she tried to explain, "but I lost it all."

I was floored. I was going to have to foot the entire bill. Somehow. How?

This was our first company dispute.

A few days later, when Heather wasn't around and I was still fuming, my son, Sean, actually backed up Heather's stance, affirming that twenty-five hundred dollars was indeed a reasonable price for the work she had commissioned. As Sean held a degree in art and had a good handle on design and printing costs, I conceded that maybe he was right. Which meant Heather was, too. I felt guilty for becoming so upset and apologized to her.

Begrudgingly, and by making arrangements to pay in installments, the bill was finally paid. I forwarded the nutritional information the food lab had worked up to our printer. Luckily, he was already quite familiar with the complex F.D.A. regulations and understood exactly what was needed and typeset the labels accordingly. That's one worry off my list.

The silver lining was when they finally arrived. The new labels made my job so much easier. Blistered fingers from cutting out the shape of the state of Oregon late into the night was a part of my past now, thank God.

And although I didn't admit it to Heather at the time, I really was delighted with the design and copy. For several months, I kept waiting for the other shoe to drop. I worried that the F.D.A. would contact us and tell us our labels were somehow not in compliance with their regulations but we never heard from them at all so I was left to surmise that no news is good news and my fears just sort of faded away as a distant memory.

As our orders and territory grew, we needed special-sized case boxes to hold larger orders of the chai safely. Naturally, they were unavailable as stock boxes, so we would have to custom manufacture boxes to suit our packaging dimensions. And that required more capital. And we needed several hundred case boxes. Before we could move forward.

We were stuck in a Catch-22: we couldn't afford to buy the boxes until after we had used the boxes to deliver the chai to our customers. Our customers, obviously, wouldn't pay our accounts payable invoice until they had received our product - and sometimes not until thirty to ninety days later. But we couldn't get the product to them without first paying to manufacture the custom case boxes - which we couldn't afford until we got paid from our accounts receivables for the chai we delivered to them which they wouldn't pay until...it was a vicious cycle.

I phoned my niece, knowing that her boyfriend's father owned a custom box manufacturing facility in Canby, Oregon. I was hoping I could network the family connection for a better than market deal on the boxes or at least finesse some grace time in paying for them.

"Don't worry about the bill," my niece offered, "You can pay for the boxes later."

I was thankful and relieved. I had no idea where that money would have come from. Six weeks after their delivery, I was still unsure where the money was coming from. The bill amounted to just under three hundred dollars, an insignificant amount but I just couldn't scrape it together. Fortunately, my sister, Merre, came to our rescue and paid our bill in full.

A few days later, I introduced my sister-in-law, Carol, to our chai and our new company.

"What do you think?" I asked.

"It's great." She said, "but are you prepared to be successful, Tedde? I can see this thing taking over your lives."

I was so caught up in this new adventure and so busy with all the immediate urgencies of our everyday demands that I hadn't given a lot of thought to the future I was hustling so hard to manifest. Why was I doing this? Was this what I wanted? Had I just gotten swept up in Heather's dream? Caught in the momentum of her enthusiasm? Like everyone else she managed to convince to fall in love with her product? Could we really be successful with our little endeavor? Would we fall flat on our faces? The possibility that it might actually be wildly successful just never occurred to me.

Carol continued, "What was David's reaction?"

"Benign skepticism." I chuckled. Still lost in thought considering the flurry of doubts and issues her question had raised, I tried to focus and more fully answer her question: "I think he'd prefer I just get another job rather than start a business but he's not standing in our way. He knows I'm a hard worker. But to him, this would be just another one of my little "side" businesses - none of which have ever really taken off - and this doesn't promise to be any different."

"It takes focus and determination to succeed," I continued, as much a pep lecture to myself as an answer to Carol. "Heather certainly has those qualities in abundance. She's highly energetic: she runs up to eleven miles a day. I know that Heather will work hard, especially if she's committed to the project. And there was no doubt that she's passionate about her chai."

"But it's harder for you," Carol read my mind.

"I have the energy," I rationalized, "but what if we go bankrupt? What if Heather quits her masters program - and then we fail?" I was really worried my daughter and I might be going down a disastrous dead-end path.

"Write affirmations and visualize success," Carol suggested. "It'll help you overcome your fears. It works for me."

It sounded like a good idea. I wrote pages and pages of: "Oregon Chai is a successful company. Oregon Chai is a successful company. Oregon Chai is a successful company. Oregon Chai is a successful company..." And soon, even I believed.

That same fall, Carol gave us a critical thousand dollars to help cover our ever-increasing expenses. It seemed we were just hemorrhaging cash. When we were able, I offered to repay both Carol and Merre - but they both asked for company shares instead. At the time, none of us knew if the shares would ever be worth anything, but in retrospect, it turned out to be a very lucrative investment on their part.

I now have an enhanced appreciation for those key family and friends' loans that while perhaps minor monetarily in the grand scope of things, they were critical in terms of timing to get us through the tightest cash crunches in our fledgling stages. They very well might have been the difference between our making it or not. Fortunately for them, too, their long-term faith in us paid off ten-fold.

As we moved into the retail arena, we realized that we'd need a new sizing structure as well. We'd been selling quarts to the espresso bars for food service sales, but a quart was excessive for retail. We had used pints as samples for new customers, so we decided to repurpose the pints for retail and downsized our samples to eight-ounce bottles.

The addition of our new retail line meant brewing even more chai. I was now making two eight-gallon batches of chai at each brewing session. And double batches meant twice the spice, twice the tea and twice the honey. And twice the schlepping.

I was still hauling the containers from my car to the church basement. Worse yet, on the way out, I was lugging double the heavy, water-based chai up all those stairs and back out to my car. I felt like Mickey Mouse in The Sorcerer's Apprentice as I ran back and forth from the stove, carting steaming liquid up the stairs, down the hall and out to my car. I often dreamt about the chai overflowing from boiling cauldrons, filling the room, flooding the church's basement and out onto the parking lot, washing my new car away.

Since the business was growing so rapidly, we decided we ought to incorporate. Lori's father, George Spencer, worked as an attorney and offered us his help. One evening, the three of us met at Lori's parents' home. Both of Lori's parents liked our product and were supportive of Lori and our venture. That evening was fun. I watched Heather and Lori chat in the kitchen, giggling and animated as if they were schoolgirls again, having a great time.

With their excitement in the background, I spoke with Lori's father in the living room.

"I don't plan to stay in this venture very long," I told him. "I didn't go back to school to work in a cannery!"

We both laughed.

A few days later, my friend Carla arrived at our home for a visit. As I stood in our dining room telling her all about Oregon Chai, Carla became very excited.

"It sounds like a great adventure," she said. "I would love to join you. What do you think? Would you consider having me as your partner? Do you think we could work together?"

All of a sudden, I felt lost in a trance: everything moved in slow motion. I felt our precious friendship dangling on a precipice.

About ten years earlier, I had started another business with a friend: a small, vintage clothing boutique in downtown Portland. We scrubbed, painted and finally opened the store. After five months of hard work and long hours cleaning, mending and ironing everything we sold, my friend burned out. After a lengthy discussion about our drop in sales and some poor purchasing decisions, she became upset.

"I'm quitting the business," she said.

I was stunned. "I think you're just tired and simply need a break," I said.

"No," she persisted, "I want out."

She consulted an attorney and demanded that I pay her for her time. I couldn't understand how that was possibly fair or even legal. She was my business partner and if there had been any money to be paying either one of us, we wouldn't even have been having this conversation. I had spent as much time starting our business as she had and I'd paid all the expenses. She hadn't invested a dime. Besides, why did she deserve to be paid? She was the one walking out on me. I felt betrayed. Taken advantage of. But, despite all the financial disagreements and the arguments, in the end, the worst part of all, was that I had lost one of my best friends.

These events flashed through my mind as I stared dumbfounded at my eager friend Carla. We had enjoyed a twenty-five year friendship that began before Heather was even born. She'd babysat my children, visited my home innumerable times. I considered her one of my closest friends. I couldn't bear jeopardizing that. But she really wanted to join us - and I really needed the help.

I stood there thinking: she has no idea what she's in for. She couldn't possibly comprehend the manual labor and emotional stress she was volunteering for. No one had any clue how hard we were working - and none of us were getting paid or knew if there was any light at the end of the tunnel.

I was making sixteen gallons of chai twice a week - and hauling it up and down all those stairs. I was physically exhausted - but I knew I was going to need help sooner or later. And, regardless of my fears that it would ruin our friendship, Carla and I got along well and I would love to have company for all those long, lonely hours brewing the tea. Maybe some friendships can endure being in business together? Just because a past venture ruined one friendship, I thought, it didn't mean it would necessarily ruin another...did it?

"I really want to help," she reiterated, interrupting the thoughts swirling in my head.

She was a hard worker. I knew that. And she was resourceful and her interest was genuine.

"Well," I said finally, "if it's okay with Heather and Lori, it's great by me."

Carla was elated.

Lori and Heather eagerly agreed, thrilled to have more help on board. Carla worked for a dentist scheduling appointments and doing all sorts of bookkeeping. She was dependable and would stick with a task until its completion. She triple-checked everything to make sure she was correct. She worked four days a week for the dentist and then, on her precious days off and in the evenings, she helped me manufacture Oregon Chai. As we grew, we agreed, she would manage our accounting department.

Carla joined us just in time for our incorporation on October 19th, 1994. Lori's father, George, helped us develop our agreement and divide up the percentages of ownership. It was an arduous decision. Because it was her idea and her vision, I felt Heather should have the majority of stock. Also, Heather and I had worked together for several months before Lori and Carla had come on board. We had solidified the recipe, found suppliers, developed a sales strategy and set up all the basic business procedures and jumped through all the governmental hoops, so we both believed we should hold a majority of the company's shares.

On the other hand, Lori and Carla were willing to work hard - and no one was getting paid. If the company failed, it wouldn't matter how many shares any of us held. But if we succeeded, there ought to be plenty to go around. We finally arrived at the decision that Heather should have the majority of stock, followed by me, then Lori, and finally, Carla, who had just come on board.

Heather in Himalayas, 1989

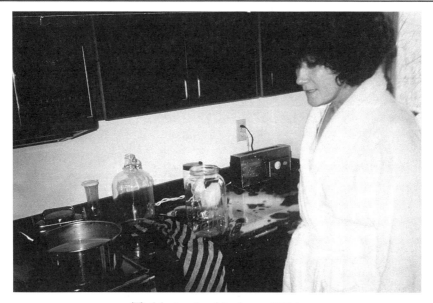

Tedde in the kitchen, 1994

Tedde unloading her Ford Escort in front
of Sunset Family Church, 1994

Heather's original logo design, 1994

First professionally designed
marketing material, 1994

SECTION II:

Into Boiling Water

C H A P T E R 5

Going Pro

By now, our business was sprinting along so rapidly it was all we could do to hang on. One afternoon, while Carla and I were brewing at the church, which we did consistently twice a week now, Heather darted in, out of breath, more excited than I'd ever seen her.

"They're asking for something less sweet! You need to make one less sweet!" she said. "They also want a decaffeinated concentrate. And a less sweet decaffeinated version," she added.

And she sprinted out the door. I glanced over at Carla, who was standing next to a huge pot of steaming chai. She stared back at me with a look of bewilderment. We could barely keep up with brewing one recipe. How on earth were we going to manage to keep up with four different variations?

Heather's original concept for Oregon Chai was a sweet, spicy tea latte based nearly entirely on flavor - with the amount of honey a key element. We had never even thought beyond this basic formula. But Heather was the one who spoke with our customers on a daily basis - she had her finger on the pulse of our marketplace - and they wanted an alternative chai - and her gut instinct was that we should accommodate what they wanted.

I'd done my own unofficial focus group testing and most people, when given a choice, always preferred a sweeter chai. In my heart, I wasn't certain this was a good idea. Would the market be large enough? I wondered. Would it support the additional costs? In the end, Heather's confidence, strengthened by the fact that Oregon Chai was her vision, persuaded me.

Most of our products were distributed through natural food stores and their customers were definitely more particular about processed food ingredients than the average consumer. Sugar and caffeine were considered unhealthy and avoided by many of our health-conscious consumers. Even though the amount of caffeine in our chai was small compared to coffee and soft drinks, I knew a decaffeinated concentrate would be a good enhancement to our product line. A less-sweet version also seemed to be a good modification to pursue because so many diabetics can't tolerate products with sugar and dieters try to avoid it. If nothing else, these line extensions promised to open up new markets for us.

"Can we support four recipe versions?" I asked Carla, the other half of Oregon Chai's manufacturing department. "It would mean different labels, additional setup fees and plate costs. And how much less sweet? How do we determine the level of sweetness and decide how much less honey to use?"

"I don't know," she said.

We were both baffled.

But before we knew it, we were producing four distinct chai concentrate variations: our original, and decaffeinated, less-sweet and less-sweet decaffeinated, all packaged in four different sizes: half-gallons, quarts, pints and half-pints - so sixteen variations.

Heather's relentless sales efforts flooded Carla and I with orders. We were overwhelmed. We could barely keep up. Carla even quit her full-time job which was a major step for her as she and her husband relied on her income and we still couldn't afford to pay her - but there was no way we could've kept up with our production demands without her full-time help.

We doubled our time at the church kitchen. We went from two days a week to four days a week - which was as much as they could possibly spare - they were, after all, still a church, with their own activities and demands for their own property.

In our current facilities, we could only make sixteen gallons at a time. My arms ached from pouring. My wrists stung from twisting caps. My back throbbed from heaving fully packed boxes of chai up and down the length of those two ever-increasing flights of stairs. I was exhausted. I knew we needed a better, faster method for brewing our chai. We had simply outgrown the church's kitchen.

I began exploring the possibility of purchasing our own equipment. But while that made perfect cost-effective sense, it was a pipe dream considering our financial situation. Just the kettles themselves cost anywhere from $2,500 to $6,000 - and we didn't have anywhere near that kind of cash - not to mention that that was only one piece of the puzzle. I looked at used equipment but the cost was still too high. But I was determined to find a better solution. I searched until I finally located a couple of two-hundred-gallon used kettles at a reasonable price. Would these be a prudent investment? Were these the right size to commit to if we purchased them? I wondered. I did some quick calculations in my head.

Let's see, I thought. We're producing sixteen gallons of concentrate four days a week. That adds up to sixty-four gallons a week. And this production rate is after just a couple of months of being in business. How fast will we outgrow these kettles? What will our growth rate be? If I purchase fifty-gallon kettles, how long will it be before we need the two-hundred-gallon kettles and how long will those last? The questions tumbled through my head.

We'll also need bottling equipment...and a building! I thought.

I started hunting with the single-mindedness of a ravenous tiger.

Carla discovered a facility about fifty miles outside of Portland. Its previous owner had financed its construction with a grant from the Oregon Lottery. She had planned on producing canned milk for export but had never finished the project. The building was brand new, ready and available. It was the ideal set-up: one mammoth room. But if we lease the building, I thought, next we'll need to hire people to handle production. I knew nothing about the equipment and certainly wouldn't know what to do if any of it failed. I continued weighing our options. Using what little cash we had wisely was imperative. We couldn't afford a wrong decision.

I looked for ways to cut costs everywhere. I found a specialty store where I discovered spices in larger quantities at wholesale prices.

I was delighted with their selection. They had hundreds of spices hanging from racks on the wall or piled on shelves. Not a gourmet cook, I knew nothing about spices. There were so many shapes, sizes and colors that I was completely baffled. I delighted at finding a bright pink pepper. I marveled at an anise shaped like a strange star. I had never seen anything like them. I breathed in each spice, dreaming of how we might use them. The store was warm and nurturing. It was truly intoxicating. It was Nirvana to me.

"Hi there," a clerk said as she approached me. "How can I help you?"

"Hi, I need information on your wholesale pricing," I said.

"Our pricing is based on volume and weight. The more you buy, the better the price. We want to sell our inventory as quickly as possible so the spices don't just sit on the shelves and lose their flavor."

The staff at this specialty shop was knowledgeable and supportive and ensured that my orders were filled in a timely manner. They helped keep my fears of failure at bay. "Oregon Chai is a successful company, Oregon Chai is a successful company..." I would will it so.

One of the owners of the company suggested we switch from vanilla extract to fresh vanilla bean after explaining that recovering alcoholics often avoid beverages made with extracts because of their alcohol content. This sounded like an excellent idea, so I implemented it immediately. It turned out that the fresh vanilla greatly improved our chai, it was so much more flavorful.

One day while picking up an order, I met another wholesale customer. A tall, lanky man with graying hair stood next to me as we each waited for our spices.

"Do you make your products yourself? Or do you outsource?" I asked him, still considering leasing the building Carla had seen earlier that week.

"I use a small, local producer who makes products for other people," he said and gave me the contact information for this referral.

I spoke with the producer and was invited to meet with them and tour their plant. The facility was located amid a small industrial complex. Upon entering their warehouse, I saw a two-hundred-gallon kettle, one fifty-gallon kettle and bottling equipment. It looked perfect. Relief is in sight, I thought. We could produce greater volumes of chai without the immense capital outlay required to buy the equipment ourselves.

I made the decision on the spot to begin using this production facility immediately. And we were lucky that I did. Within a year, we went from making sixty-four gallons of chai a week to five thousand gallons of chai a day. And by January of 1998, we'd increased to thirty-five thousand gallons at each production run.

Our attorney drew up a manufacturing agreement, including a non-disclosure statement so that our formula would remain secret. On my next visit to the production facility, I shared our freshly-penned agreement with the owner.

As she read the contract, her face grew taught. Her lips thinned. She gritted her teeth. Her posture morphed from easy relaxation to tension. She leaned forward and pressed her forearms into the edge of her desk.

"I'm not going to sign a document like this with a bunch of legalese," she said. "I'm a professional - an honest person. I'm as good as my word!"

She's going to throw the paper at me, I thought - but she just tossed it onto her desk.

I was astonished. I had no idea how to proceed. We needed her help desperately and, so far, I hadn't found any decent alternatives. I'd spoken with several other processors but none of them could help us. They were all either too big and wouldn't bother with an insignificant run of two hundred gallons or they packed only wide-mouthed containers. None of them would handle plastic bottles. This just has to work, I thought.

"I have recipes on file for all of my customers," she said, bringing me back from my reverie. "I'd be out of business if I divulged anyone's formula. Your information will be stored separately from everyone else's information. None of my other customers will have access to it. Everything will be destroyed if we stop making your product."

I could see she was adamant but I tried to convince her - this was really important to us.

"The contract is just a formality," I said, "a standard for this type of relationship. Asking you to sign it is no reflection on your character..."

She wouldn't budge.

We needed help urgently. That's all there was to it. Her way or the highway. I didn't feel like I had a choice.

"Okay," I said. "No agreement. We'll hire you without one."

Our new production arrangement required that we convert our formula from teaspoons and cups into grams and pounds. Carla, Heather and I arrived at their plant armed with our teaspoons, ready for the conversion. Measuring out a teaspoon of spice, we either weighed it or counted out the whole spices and weighed them.

When we finished weighing all of our ingredients, our formula was adapted from weights to percentages. Once the new formula was ready, I ordered the necessary supplies and spices. No more counting individual teabags, either - we now purchased and weighed loose bulk tea.

Before the conversion, I would buy our honey in plastic half-gallon jugs. But our new manufacturer insisted these were insufficient: we'd outgrown the small jugs. Now we needed honey in bulk, too. So I phoned a wholesale honey supplier.

I leafed through their catalog and noticed they offered several pages of different types of honey. I'd never seen so many varieties in all my life.

I had no idea so many even existed since all I'd ever seen at my grocery store or Costco was one kind. I was confused. I had no idea which to buy, so I asked their customer service representative for help.

"I've never heard of chai," she said. "I really can't tell you which honey would work best."

"Okay, well honey is honey, I guess," I said and I bought the least expensive one.

"It should work fine," the rep assured me.

That turned out to be a huge mistake. I didn't know it at the time, but my first lesson in quality control loomed on the horizon.

We also now needed larger quantities of containers. So the search began for a new vendor. I explored our options and found a supply company that sold everything anyone could possibly need for a small business. Perfect, I thought: we can buy whatever we'll need in small quantities but at large-quantity discounts. Great.

Next, we needed larger teabags. Much larger. We needed teabags the size of pillowcases, to be exact, which of course, no one makes. So, on a whim, I ventured out to a local fabric store and searched for some way to make them myself. I wasn't quite sure what I was looking for so I started near the polyesters. I was overwhelmed by the selection.

"Can I help you?" I heard a voice say from behind me.

"Yes," I said. "I'm looking for some fabric that I can use to make huge teabags."

"Really?" she asked, incredulous, highly entertained by the thought.

"Yes, really!" I said.

She giggled (she must have thought I drank tons of tea). She led me over to the bridal fabrics and we found some lovely white nylon fabric that looked ideal: porous enough to let the water through yet dense enough so that the tealeaves wouldn't slip into the brew.

Few Americans had ever heard of chai, which was a blessing for us. It made us newsworthy. Since we had zero budget for advertising, we scrambled to secure our exposure via press coverage.

As one of the first - and still one of the very few - chai companies operating within the United States, we were fortunate to hit the market with a new and exciting product with perfect timing. Add to that Heather's interesting story of discovery and our rare and newsworthy team of two generations of four female friends, that included a mother and a daughter - and we quickly became media darlings.

On Halloween, 1994, we composed our first press release - a simple one-page description of our company and our product - and submitted it to local and regional papers. About a week later, on 11/8/94, we were thrilled to open up The Daily Journal of Commerce praising Oregon Chai as "a hot investment prospect" alongside a photograph of Heather smiling, holding a steaming cup of chai.

The power of feature articles hit home to us. They are simply head and shoulders above paid advertising in terms of effectiveness and reach. They are more credible and infinitely more engaging and evergreen. We used that article for a decade, though there were many, many more to come.

C H A P T E R   6

What's Honey Got To Do, Got To Do With It?

I still remember November 11, 1994 like it was the proverbial yesterday: it was our first co-packer production day for Oregon Chai.

I had an intense cold. I felt so ill, I was certain I had bronchitis - but the show must go on. We had worked so hard to get to this point that no matter how bad I felt, there was no way I was going to miss the first processor manufacturing of our Oregon Chai. It was exciting. A triumph, even.

Carla and I arrived early that morning and donned hairnets and white lab coats. We waited anxiously in the office while the production crew filled the kettle with water and brought it to a boil.

The production manager carefully weighed the spices according to our measurements. She ground the ginger and the vanilla beans in a food processor. The vanilla beans were a terrible mess. They became stringy and eventually had to just be cut by hand.

I felt giddy. It was such fun sitting in her office while someone else did all the work. I also felt a little guilty, just sitting there, merely waiting for them to bring me a sample to taste. But I was relieved, content to sit back, relax and enjoy the experience. No more sore muscles. No more hours of lugging chai up two flights of stairs. We now had professional, experienced manufacturers. I felt confident that every batch of Oregon Chai from now on would be as consistently delicious as our customers had come to expect.

"This is such a beautiful process to watch," I said to Carla, "making a delicious drink out of such wonderful and diverse ingredients."

After the brew had fully steeped, they brought us our first taste. I couldn't wait to try it. They told us that we should always sample the product in the same cup so our quality control testing would never be thrown off by a different feel, taste or smell from the variation in factors other than the product. The only element any of us wanted to pay attention to was the actual chai itself.

Five of the workers tasted the product along with us and all of them liked it but it tasted a bit different to me. The color was darker than the countless batches I'd made from scratch. But, I rationalized: it must just be a natural variation. This was, after all, an entirely different process. It was a larger scale brewing method, we had changed the volume of ingredients, so its inevitably going to appear, taste and smell different, I rationalized. I suppressed my reservations conceding the taste was within an acceptable range.

"You've got a tiger by the tail here," the owner said.

After brewing, each bottle was filled using mechanized bottling equipment. I was in awe. The lids still had to be attached by hand, however. The containers were blisteringly hot which made them difficult to hold and cap, slowing the process down.

And the ever-annoying labels persisted in giving us grief.

Our brand new labels had been printed on flat pieces of paper called "crack-and-peel" and even though my tediously cutting out of hundreds of little Oregon shapes was thankfully a part of my past, bending the labels and feeling for the perforations to peel off the backs was still too laborious a process. The plant owner insisted we'd purchased the wrong type.

I made a mental note to check into our other options, weary of this incessant burr in my side.

After our production, there was a significant amount of ginger left over.

"What should we do with this?" the production supervisor asked me.

"You can just throw it out," I answered. "We always use fresh ginger."

"Why don't you just freeze it for next time?" she asked.

I was unsure but she assured me: "It'll be fine."

Everything was going so well and since we were now working with industry professionals, I thought, why not? We wrapped the ginger carefully in paper, placed it in a box and put it into the freezer. I drove home satisfied with our work, thrilled that we had just brewed one hundred and eighty-five gallons in one brewing session and had sixty cases of chai ready to go out to our ever-growing market.

I did some more research on the labels and discovered, not surprisingly, that the plant owner was right. There were labels we could print that came on rolls designed to fit automatic labeling machines that would save the workers a great deal of time. Who knew? Obviously, that was the type we should be using. They were more expensive labels to be sure, but there was no comparison when you calculated the savings they translated into by significantly lowering our equipment rental and labor costs. Why is it, I thought, that we have to learn each and every lesson the hard way?

At six p.m. that night, I was scheduled at Nature's in Beaverton to provide consumer samples of Oregon Chai. My sister, Merre, volunteered to help me out.

We set up a small table at the end of one of the store's aisles with an elegant silver tray holding the cups. I mixed and heated the chai in their deli, poured it into a thermal pitcher to retain its heat and waited anxiously for their customers. I was happy - everything was going so well. For the first time ever, I didn't even bother to taste the chai. But that didn't last long.

As the store customers sampled our product, they avoided making eye contact with me, which was really odd because I'd become so accustomed to people smiling and raving about our chai.

"Hmm," they'd usually say with a suspicious look. "What is it?"

"It's really delicious," I'd say. "You'll like it!"

Some would lift the cup cautiously, hold it to their lips and sniff.

"It smells good," they'd comment and slowly take a sip. As they swallowed, they would glance up, their eyes would widen and a smile would evolve on their faces.

"Oh, this is good!" was the typical comment.

But not tonight.

Tonight, the response was uniformly negative. An aberration to be sure. The patrons would peer around awkwardly, mumble something unintelligible without looking at either of us and quickly plunk their half-full cups onto any available ledge and get out of there as fast as they could. What's happening? I wondered nervously.

"Something isn't right," I whispered to Merre.

I peered into the cup I was holding. The color was peculiar, sort of gray, like the color white laundry fades to after too many washings. That's odd, I thought. Really weird. I took a sip. It was horrible! I was distraught, beside myself. I didn't know what to do.

"Tedde," Merre whispered. "You need to go outside and get some air, take a walk."

Though I've always considered myself a bit controlling, keeping my emotions in check has always been difficult for me. Honoring my sister's suggestion, I stepped outside for a few moments to collect myself and think. What's wrong with the chai? I couldn't even imagine. When I came back inside, Merre had sold a couple of bottles.

"You sold this stuff?" I asked, incredulously, realizing she could sell ice to Eskimos.

"Don't worry, I gave them the good chai you and Carla made from scratch at the church," she whispered.

That was simultaneously the good news and the bad news. I was relieved no one was going home with this disgusting crap passing itself off as our amazing chai but on the other hand, what on earth had we just paid all that money for? What was wrong with our hundred and eighty gallons of chai? Sixty cases! We had hired professionals, after all.

I wandered the store aisles trying to get my emotions in check but the grimaced faces of the taste-testing patrons swirled in my mind. I had to figure out what had gone wrong.

I examined the new professionally packaged bottle of chai in comparison to one of the older bottles of chai concentrate that Carla and I had brewed at the church. The plant-bottled one was a bizarre greenish-black and quite frankly, foul-smelling.

As I reeled, trying to figure out the problem, a few of the deli attendants offered to taste the new product.

"It's interesting," one of them said unconvincingly.

Another one took a sip: "Oh, umm, sort of tastes like flowers."

That's kind, I thought. More like fertilizer, if you want to be more specific.

"This isn't our chai," a third offered from behind the counter. "I mean, this doesn't even look like the Oregon Chai we've been selling."

She pointed to the older, church-brewed bottle of chai sitting on the table. "This is our chai. See? Ours is brown. That stuff is black."

She was right!

Our fresh, professionally manufactured product looked like the dregs of day-old coffee left ignored to burn in a coffee pot. I tasted it without the milk.

"It's sour!" I said, still trying to make sense of the situation.

It was not the wonderful flavor I loved and not even the slightly off chai I'd tasted earlier that day. Something had changed. And whatever it was, it was getting worse every minute.

I grabbed another container. It, too, was sour with the same rancid, day-old-coffee consistency. The bottom fell out of my stomach. The blood drained from my face, pooling down into my toes. My body fell into shock. I stood, paralyzed. I couldn't move.

Think! I admonished myself. The chai had tasted great that morning. It had smelled fine. I had noticed that the color was a bit off but when we blended it with milk, it looked acceptable. How could it go from the luscious brown brew that we had sampled just a few hours ago to this sour, odorous stuff? I took several deep breaths, gathered up the supplies - including the dregs from the deli counter - and dragged my unwilling legs back to our demo table.

My sister was still handing out customer samples. Panic set in.

"This is good, I'll take a bottle," I heard one customer say.

I couldn't believe it. They were giggling, my sister and the store customers, enjoying that foul stuff. Merre sold four more bottles. Now that's salesmanship, I thought, certainly not a reflection of the batch's quality.

I just wanted to grab my stuff, duck my head and run as fast as I could out the nearest door. I yearned to jump into my car, speed home, throw on my jammies and hide under my down quilt, hoping I'd wake up and realize it was all just a bad dream.

"Let's stay," she said as I gathered my nerve and returned to our table.

"It's fine," she consoled me, trying to make the best of the situation.

"They don't know the difference. We have to sell it all."

But I knew.

"We can't sell this," I said.

"You have to recoup your losses," she said.

But I was adamant. I didn't want this cast-off representing itself as Oregon Chai.

"If people taste this, very few will ever buy our product again," I said, firmly, half a lecture to myself.

"It will kill any hopes we have of them ever actually trying our real Oregon Chai again," I explained. "It will do us more damage to stay than to go. We have to leave. Immediately."

Persistent Merre held her ground. What luck did I have to be surrounded by so many persistent women?

But finally, she acquiesced.

"You're right," she said. "We really should leave. Besides, you look awful - especially when people tried the chai!" She laughed.

"I'm sure I grimaced as they drank it," I said. "I was afraid it might poison them!"

We high tailed it out of there, corralling every last sample into our protective custody.

That evening I phoned our manufacturer and my partners.

Since the 185 gallons of chai we had just manufactured were essentially garbage, we needed more chai to fill our waiting orders - and fast. But it was a weekend - and the production crew was gone. And no one quite knew what the problem was, so who's to say we wouldn't just replicate it all over again?

The owner agreed to let us use her plant while they were closed but she mandated that we only use the smaller fifty-gallon kettle as none of us had any experience using the larger kettle. Consequently, we couldn't produce as much chai as the full plant could when properly manned - but it was enough to get us through this hump.

But how will we pay for it? I wondered. We certainly couldn't absorb a mistake of this magnitude. Our cash was running dangerously low. Carla and I had both invested everything we had. Fortunately for us, my husband never complained. But Carla wasn't as lucky.

"Don't invest all of your savings in a new business with an unknown product," an old friend and neighbor of Carla's warned her one night. "It's too risky. You're making a huge mistake."

Carla and I had covered nearly all the expenses out of pocket up until this point. And now we'd hit that infamous crossroads where you have to decide if you're throwing good money after bad. Was it false economy to keep pouring our savings into this venture to continually work for free? Were we stupid? Would it ever pay off?

We both felt we had no choice but to stick with it. Somehow, Carla and I pooled our resources with the little cash we'd accumulated in the company bank account and purchased a duplicate set of bulk ingredients and supplies to repeat the exercise. We knew we just had to keep going - whatever it took.

Since it was a weekend and we didn't have time to wait for wholesale orders to be filled by our suppliers, I raced over to Costco remembering they stocked half-gallons of honey. I grabbed as many as my cart would hold, piling them one on top of the other. I tried to ignore the stares as

I shoved that heavy pushcart toward the checkout stand.

"Gee, you must really have a sweet tooth!" I overheard.

Everybody's a comedian.

I chuckled apologetically, just trying to make my way through the line to make my ridiculous purchase. But in my heart, I just wanted to tell them all about Oregon Chai - how great it was, how Heather discovered it, how fast we were growing, how proud I was of our company in spite of all our trials and tribulations - but I didn't have the time. The brewing was waiting. We needed more chai ASAP. I ignored the stares and snickers and struggled to get my colossal load through the parking lot and into my car.

The confusingly rancid chai had to be dumped and fresh, new chai produced. Fortunately, a few of our family members volunteered their help. With thumping rock music blaring in the background, Carla and I brewed fresh, flavorful chai while a handful of relatives chucked the spoiled chai down the drain. Two of my nephews happily leaped onto the emptied containers to flatten them and heaved them into a dumpster.

Since we were untrained in using the automatic bottle-filling equipment, our husbands poured the fresh chai out of half-gallon pitchers into the bottles then fastened the lids by hand. They stuck the labels on and packed the finished chai into our custom case boxes.

When we were through, we realized the plant floor was covered with sweet, sticky chai that had probably squirted out as the plastic bottles were flattened or spilled as our husbands had filled the bottles one by one - or, most likely, both. We sprayed the floor and every surface down with a huge, black hose and swabbed the floor. When the plant was tidy and all of our supplies were tucked away, I hugged and thanked everyone for their help. Then we all headed home for some much-needed rest. In spite of her utter exhaustion, Carla ferried all the ingredients home that night, determined to figure out what had gone wrong, and made a gallon of chai in her kitchen. She tested and examined each ingredient one by one and surmised the problem stemmed from the bulk honey - the only ingredient change.

She called me on the phone: "Everything was just the same as always until I added the new bulk honey," she explained. "After I added the honey, the chai started getting darker and darker and started to smell funny."

I was baffled.

"By the time I'd gotten it into the bottle," she said, "it was disgusting."

"I wonder why we didn't notice it before?" I asked.

"It was probably fine when we tasted and bottled it," she explained. ""It took quite awhile for the reaction."

The following day, Carla called the honey supplier and asked them if they had any idea what had happened.

"You probably bought the wrong kind of honey," they hypothesized. "Baker's Amber is a poor quality honey. You should have used clover or alfalfa honey."

I had had no idea that it mattered. And no one at the supplier had told me either. They hadn't had any idea what chai even was. It dawned on me they probably had no idea it was a food product.

That night Heather, Lori, Carla and I gathered at my house. We tasted the foul-smelling chai.

"It tastes like salsa," Heather insisted.

"That makes no sense," I dismissed her comment, not remotely interested in anyone's analysis of our taste profile at this stage of the game if it didn't relate to our pressing honey fiasco.

In my kitchen, we brewed a fresh gallon of chai and divided it into four quarts, testing a different type of honey in each batch. The results were interesting: three of the honeys were fine. But as we sat observing our experiment like four scientists discovering a new species, we watched the chai with the cheap bulk Baker's Amber honey gradually turn black. But, like Carla had reported, it was not immediate: the discoloration only occurred after it sat awhile. What's happening? I wondered.

Carla phoned the supplier again. They offered no explanation. We had to have an answer. So I phoned our supplier and explained our situation.

"Do you know what went wrong?" I asked. "Or how we can protect ourselves from this happening again?" We certainly couldn't afford another mishap.

"You'll have to bring us a sample and we'll have a look at it," the representative advised.

The next day, I delivered a sample of our malodorous chai along with a sample of freshly brewed chai - but never heard from them again. So much for helping us, I thought. I was frustrated and demanded a resolution. I sought help elsewhere.

I called the American Honey Board in Washington, D.C. A representative there vaguely remembered hearing about a similar situation from several years back. She tracked down the name and number of a Washington state beekeeper who had published an article about the problem. I called him immediately.

"Oh," he said, remembering, "You probably got Chinese honey. In China, they have modern factories for processing honey but the beekeeping farms the honey originates from are quite primitive. One beekeeper might scrape the honey from the hive on a daily basis, thinking that'll increase his output, but it doesn't allow the bees to completely refine the honey, so it dries out."

"Also," he went on, "they scrape so close to the hive that they run the risk of getting eggs and larvae in the honey. This can cause impurities and, in some instances, it can cause tea to turn into vinegar. That's probably what happened with your chai," he said. "Chinese honey is the cheapest grade."

I was alarmed. How could we not have known about this? I couldn't believe it. Why hadn't our supplier told us this?

And then it struck me: I had bought the least expensive honey I could find. I didn't think it mattered. They hadn't told me it was imported (not that I would have known that was an issue). I promised myself: we will never use anything but domestic honey from this point on.

After we concluded our discussion, I phoned Costco's honey supplier.

"Do you sell honey in bulk?" I asked. "I need fifty-gallon drums."

"Yes, we do," the representative answered.

"Where does it come from?" I asked.

"Well," she said, "eighty percent comes from North Dakota and Montana and twenty percent comes from the state of Washington. It's from clover, alfalfa and flowers. But clover doesn't grow in Washington anymore."

"Hmm, my uncle told me the same thing," I said, remembering that my uncle had worked as a wheat rancher in northeastern Washington and years ago, his tractor had required a special attachment on its front so that he could shear down clover that grew in excess of eight feet, but now that was no longer necessary.

"Do you know why it doesn't grow there any longer?" I asked.

"That clover only grows every other year," she explained. "The seed has a very hard hull and the conditions need to be perfect for it to germinate. It can't be too cold or too hot, too wet or too dry."

This jived with what my uncle had told me. She went on.

"Farmers now use herbicides that kill broad-leaf plants," she said, "but the federal government is working to change the regulations on the usage of these herbicides and those measures will likely protect the clover in the future."

"Will the clover ever come back?" I asked.

"Maybe," she said. "But it may need to be reseeded."

All of this affected the price of honey, which in turn affected my decision to purchase an inferior product. Again, I thought, always learning the hard way - isn't there a way around the old fashioned school of hard knocks?

Every day we received more and more orders for Oregon Chai. I felt it important that we fill them in a timely manner. I was concerned that if we ran out of chai, our retailers might feel that they could not depend on us and might eventually seek other suppliers, now that we were beginning to attract competitors. Remaining trustworthy and reliable became our primary goal.

Just two days after this nightmare, on 11/13/94, The Oregonian, unaware of our fiasco, ran a very complimentary article about us. The columnist shared Heather's discovery of chai high in the Himalayas. He joked in his article that Oregon Chai was just "not the same without the buffalo milk and goat brains on the side." The article couldn't have had better timing to raise our spirits.

The following week, the plant made another batch of chai for us and we were back in business. I was relieved that we'd quickly turned this disaster around.

But Heather, oddly, was still convinced it tasted like salsa.

C H A P T E R   7

Tijuana Chai

The very next day Carla called me on the phone.

"Tedde," Carla said, her voice cracking, "we have a problem. This chai doesn't taste right, either!"

"Carla, don't tease," I said, sensing a joke. "That isn't funny."

Although Carla had a terrific sense of humor, she wasn't laughing.

I wasn't sure I could physically cope with the second professionally prepared batch having a problem, too.

"My son tried the chai," she explained, almost apologetically, "and he agrees with Heather. He thinks it tastes like salsa, too."

"Oh, no," I said, sick to my stomach, when will this ever end?

The next morning, we got together and as soon as it hit my lips, I knew.

It was true. Undeniable. The chai had a hot, peppery flavor - and the aftertaste was sickening. My husband tried it, too, dubbing it "Tijuana Chai."

We called our manufacturer right away and told them what was happening. Our manufacturer admitted that they did produce salsa (as well as a variety of other sauces, syrups and pickled garlic), but whenever they switched recipes, the staff cleaned and sanitized their equipment completely. There simply was no visible residue and they were confident there was no way our chai could have become contaminated.

By the time I arrived at the plant, the crew had disassembled all the equipment. The hoses running from the kettle to the bottling equipment were indeed tinted a pinkish red and smelled suspiciously like chili peppers. It reminded me of spaghetti sauce stained Tupperware.

All the equipment, including the hoses, was thoroughly cleaned after each use. It had never occurred to any of us that these hoses could be a source of contamination but since there was no other source of contamination, our manufacturer agreed this must be the origin of our problem.

"Well," the owner said, "we'll replace all of the salsa-flavored chai." And she promptly replaced all the hoses.

Great, I thought, at least we don't have to cover the cost of producing yet another replacement batch. But they went one step further: not only did they produce a fresh batch of chai at their own expense, but they also covered the cost of all the ingredients and containers, too.

On November 21, 1994, Heather released a list to local papers to inform readers where they could buy Oregon Chai in the Portland Metro-politan area. In just four months over 70 espresso bars and retail outlets were offering Oregon Chai. Most of that grueling sales work was accomplished by my 26 year old daughter who had found her path and was running down it with fortitude and all-consuming passion.

Although my focus was manufacturing, there was always overlap between our duties and responsibilities. I tried to do my part to support Heather's marketing efforts. I donated money to the National Public Radio, which got Oregon Chai a brief mention during one of their music education programs. Every bit of exposure proved priceless.

On November 24, 1994, the plant brewed a fresh new batch of replacement chai that tasted just like the Oregon Chai I had grown to love - we were - finally - back on track.

Heather was always brainstorming ways to grow our little company. One of her grander schemes was to harness the marketing and distribution power of bigger industry players. And the star player at the top of our draft wish list was Starbucks.

Starbucks did have a version of chai, but it was just spiced tea inside a teabag. Heather knew what we had was head and shoulders above their version. So, ever confident and audacious, Heather phoned Starbucks and made an appointment with its CEO.

A few days later, Heather and Lori drove to Seattle. As they arrived at the CEO's office, they were greeted warmly by his assistant then seated at an immense oval table hugged by a dozen brown leather chairs.

After a few moments, the CEO entered.

"Good afternoon," he said, extending a hand. "Tell me about your chai."

"Well," Heather said, shaking his hand. "Chai is really so much more than spiced tea. For one thing, it's very sweet and made with milk. Without milk, it's basically just spiced tea. Similar to what you're currently offering."

The conversation continued, but no offer was initiated.

"Well, I've got to run," he said after a few moments. "Thank you both so much for coming. Your product sounds wonderful."

Heather and Lori returned to Portland, excited about the meeting, yet disappointed that they hadn't closed the deal - they hadn't even been offered one or been able to propose one.

Still, Heather knew there was interest.

Meanwhile, back at home, Carla not only helped me brew the concentrate, but she also shared delivery duties with me. One Nature's that Carla delivered to stored its extra inventory in the basement. Transferring our cases down there required that we place everything on a conveyor belt at the top of the stairs, flip on a switch - and sprint down the stairs to grab the chai from the belt and set it on the basement floor before it rolled off.

During the holiday season, Carla delivered several gallons of chai to this store for their employee Christmas party. She placed the four-gallon cases onto the conveyor belt, flicked the switch and sprinted down the stairs, where she lifted the heavy cases off the treadmill belt onto the floor. The holiday season was always busy for food retailers and the area was crowded with extra stock. The conveyor belt traveled faster than Carla could keep up with. She set the first box on the floor and turned around for the second. But as she tried to grab it, like luggage moving too fast and at an awkward angle on a baggage carousel, it tipped over.

She caught it but the third box tumbled from the belt. In her attempt to seize the falling box, she missed the fourth one, which slipped off the end as well.

As she lunged for it a fifth box fell off and this one burst open. A lid flew off one of the containers and chai oozed all over the floor. Carla slipped and slid through the chai, trying to shove the remaining boxes off the belt's path. She tried to reach the switch to turn off the conveyor belt but the switch was on the far wall on the opposite side of the belt. Seeing no other alternative, Carla dove over the pile of liquid boxes, hurdling the drenched, sticky chai mess, and leaned across the belt to flip off the switch.

When she returned to our office she looked like a drowned rat. She told me: "I felt just like I Love Lucy on the chocolate line."

On December 27, 1994 our Oregon Chai logo appeared at the top of the rail on the front page of The Oregonian's FOODday section. The accompanying article featured a photo of our chai concentrate that covered half the page. It was an impressive article to be sure. What a great way to end our first year.

C H A P T E R   8

Little David Inadvertently Awakens Giant Goliath

Even though we were now a corporation and there were four of us working, we still couldn't keep up with every aspect of our new business. There was so much to be done and we had so little time to do it. We needed a business plan, a long-range plan and, most importantly: more money - always, more money.

Heather's fiancé had just graduated from law school and one of his classmates was Brian Ross. Both of them had passed the bar, but Brian didn't want to practice law. He wanted to start a business. Heather's fiancé had told Brian about Oregon Chai and Brian was intrigued. He wanted to join us. Heather liked Brian and thought we could use his help, so she asked him to meet with me.

I met Brian during an in-store sampling of our original chai at Nature's in Beaverton in January of 1995. He came into the store wearing a pink, long-sleeved, cotton Oxford shirt coupled with khaki slacks. His jet-black hair was tied back neatly in a short ponytail.

"Hi, I'm Brian," he said, extending his hand.

I liked him instantly.

He had a friendly, calming sparkle, a wonderful smile. I was amused by his enthusiasm for our project. I thought: he has no idea how much work this is, the problems we've encountered, the fact that none of us are making any money - and don't know if we ever will.

He shared with me his previous effort of trying to create a company that made spoons, forks and knives from recycled plastic. He had tried enlisting investors but had had no luck. As I continued to hand out samples to customers, he laid out his company's business plan. It was impressive.

"We could use one of these," I said, admiring it.

"I can write one for you," he said. "I can help you find financing - and apply for a small business loan."

I thought about it for a moment, knowing we had zero capital and how much easier everything would be if we had any money at all.

"There's no way we can pay you," I said. "But we can offer you stock in the company."

A few days later, Brian told us how many shares he would require to get involved. I discussed this with our attorney, who advised me that he thought Brian's asking price was too aggressive - but Brian held firm.

Allotting him the shares of stock he wanted meant dilution from the rest of us. It was yet another difficult decision, but, as before, he was taking a risk along with everyone else. If we failed, it didn't matter how much stock we gave him. And if we succeeded, there ought to be enough to go around. The stock just seemed this illusory currency with nebulous value.

We gave Brian his asking price in stock and he joined our team.

Brian brought in a computer, a phone, several filing cabinets and a fax machine for our home (now corporate) office. We arranged everything on two eight-foot tables. We stored the finished chai in my basement with the overflow going into Carla's garage. We were now five unpaid employees of Oregon Chai.

We never worried about bumping into one another. Carla and I were usually at the plant brewing chai or making deliveries while Lori worked from her home around her full-time job and Heather was always out making sales calls. We worked well together and though we each worked independently, we were all motivated for shared success.

On January 19, 1995, Heather and Lori were pictured in the local alternative newspaper, the Tonic, sipping warm chai at The Green Room, a small café in Northwest Portland.

The piece launched with a trivia question that I thought was a lot of fun:

Q: Oregon Chai is...

The multiple choice answers were:

A) A dangerous, new, martial arts academy

B) A Tantric sexual position involving twine, pulleys and Oregon Lottery 'Scratch-Its'

C) An endangered bird currently giving Oregon's loggers a big headache

D) Dyslexic for 'Oregon Chia'

E) A spicy, new tea beverage that tastes something like a pumpkin pie latte

I thought the first answer (a dangerous, new, martial arts academy) was feasible because of a couple of possible scenarios:

1) I looked like I practiced martial arts since I had numerous bruises on my arms from contending with forty-five pound cases of concentrate;

2) Carla found herself in a dangerous situation standing in a pool of wet, sticky chai, defending herself from several gallon-sized containers plummeting toward her on a fast-moving conveyer belt from the floor above;

As for the Oregon "Scratch-Its" mentioned in the second answer (a Tantric sexual position involving twine, pulleys and Oregon Lottery 'Scratch-Its'), against my better judgment, I often found myself buying lottery tickets hoping a major win would finance our next batch of chai. How did they know? Our personal lives remained fairly tame (at least as far as I knew). But then again, the three partners my daughter's age would most likely not share their sexual fantasies with me - nor would I want them to. After all, I thought, this is a respectable, family business, so we'd have to rule out answer "B".

It definitely wasn't "C" since that would describe our Northern Spotted Owl. A few conservatives may have disagreed with our green values, but even so, our sweet, spicy chai would most definitely improve their perspective.

And while endless people mispronounced it similarly as "chee-ah" or spelled it that way, dyslexic or not, "D" was incorrect, too.

That left only answer "E": A spicy, new tea beverage that tastes something like a pumpkin pie latte. Bingo. Pumpkin pie. Numerous customers often used that exact comparison to describe the unique flavor of Oregon Chai. It must have been the spices conjuring up a nostalgic aroma.

Everything had run smoothly for the past three months. I'd been brewing chai for over a year now and needed a break. With more than a little trepidation, I decided to take a vacation with my husband. But I was nervous leaving - like a new mother leaving her baby for the first time in the care of someone else.

Adding to my trepidation was that my vacation unfortunately coincided with the plant manager's vacation. This would leave her assistant in charge of manufacturing our chai. I convinced myself I was being ridiculous, thinking it couldn't be done without me. So I left.

When I returned, I noticed the color of the batch they had made in my absence was pale yellow rather than the chestnut brown we typically expected with a standard quality batch. I knew that as our volume grew, the production crew worked increasingly hard to make as much chai as quickly as possible but a watched pot doesn't boil - and you can't speed steeping. Tea has got to brew long enough at exactly the right temperature to coax the exotic flavors to blend into a rich, robust liquor. In their haste, I was certain, they had added the tea and spices to brew before the water had reached a roiling boil, resulting in weak tea and thus, the poor-quality chai I returned home to.

I discussed it with the plant owner.

"My production supervisor noticed the chai's color, too," she said, "and made the same comment."

"Well, I think it needs to be redone," I said flatly.

"Yes, yes, I agree," she said. "Especially since my own supervisor even mentioned the difference."

"I'm not sure how to handle this," I said. "I don't feel we should bear the burden alone."

The owner suggested that perhaps the problem lay with our tea supplier.

But I assured her that the tea used in this batch had come from the same lot as the tea we'd used in previous batches - and they had all turned out fine.

"We'll pay to remake the product," she said, "since it was clearly our error."

I was relieved. They discarded the product and, because the plant took responsibility for the problem, they covered the cost of replacing it. Again.

Then I spoke with the woman who was in charge of production during my absence.

"We always start with boiling water," I explained. "What temperature do you use to brew the tea?"

"We can't bring it to a roiling boil," she said, "because it spills over the sides of the kettle."

That's not acceptable. You can't make tea without boiling water. At least not good black tea. It was just as I'd suspected: the water was not hot enough.

The crew was understandably cautious and a bit leery of the hot liquid. A few weeks earlier, one of the workers had been pouring honey into the hot, brewed chai and it had splashed and hit him square in the face and eye. Still, I left it to them to figure out how to bring the water to a boil as that was obviously a critical step in our tea making process.

The production supervisor took me aside and told me she had discovered the pH was a bit higher than she was comfortable with. We tried to keep it below 4.35 to prevent the growth of toxic organisms. It was a little higher here than when we'd brewed at the church. We didn't understand why there was a difference but assumed it had something to do with the water. The production supervisor insisted we lower the pH level, suggesting we add acid to our chai. I was adamant that our chai remain as natural as possible so I phoned the food lab and asked if they had any other - better - ideas.

"You might try adding some fruit juice," they said, which sounded like a more natural alternative.

I tested several types: lemon, orange, apple and grape - and determined that white grape juice not only lowered our chai's pH, but was also all natural and nearly undetectable - it even improved the flavor a bit. Still, even though the problem was finally solved, it wasn't long before I was crying over sour grapes.

We made arrangements with various grocery stores and coffee houses to bring in carafes of fresh hot chai and serve free samples to their consumers as they shopped so they could taste it before buying the product. This customer sampling was a lot of work. It was critical, though, and we all knew it. It was one of the most immediate and cost effective ways for us to raise public awareness of our product: to get them to taste it and maybe even buy it on the spot. It helped us to generate good will, stimulate buzz and word of mouth. We knew that we just had to keep it up.

For in-store demonstrations, we always served our chai warm as the flavor was more pronounced when served hot. We also used whole milk because it had a richer taste and indulgent texture.

Our biggest obstacle to these in-store demonstrations was heating the chai and keeping it hot without burning it. Which we learned the hard way - once again! One afternoon, as Heather and I were handing out samples at Elephants, a delicatessen in northwest Portland, we encountered a problem. I'd purchased a thirty-cup coffee maker to heat the chai. I had blended the chai and the milk in the coffee pot and plugged it in. Everything was going fine. We chatted with customers as they sipped our warm chai. We were having a great time. Then we noticed a peculiar odor drifting throughout the store.

"Do you smell that, Heather?" I asked.

"Yes. It smells like something's burning," she said, sniffing the air.

Just then, a man walked up and tasted one of our samples. As he sipped, we watched for the usual pleased reaction. But no surprised smile appeared.

"It tastes burned," he said.

Why we hadn't considered the odor might be coming from our chai, I don't know. It had just never happened before. We took the lid off the coffee maker and just as the customer had said, it was burned.

Heather and I felt awful. We switched off the pot, poured out the ruined chai and tried to air out the space as best we could. We apologized profusely to the deli's staff and their customers. Luckily, everyone understood and the deli's business didn't suffer. Customers stayed - and some even ordered our chai.

After our chai scalded that day, I remembered my earlier reservations about heating it in coffee makers: if it wasn't circulating, I supposed, the chai would just sit on the coffee maker's element and scald. Later, when I returned home, I tried scrubbing the coffeemaker, but removing the seared chai from the pot was impossible. Our shiny new coffee maker was rubbish.

We needed another, more reliable method for sampling our chai. For small venues, we could simply heat a couple of quarts of chai on a stove and keep it warm for several hours inside one of those thermal hot pots. Customers could even serve themselves. But we were growing rapidly and we needed a better solution - fast. I couldn't lug my enormous gas range to samplings. We needed a way to heat the chai on site. It took us a few months and some extensive research on Brian's part before we discovered portable machines that could heat or cool a gallon or more of chai and keep it circulating so that each and every sample tasted perfect.

Beyond manufacturing, I tried to help Heather in her ceaseless efforts to drum up business.

When my sister and I had owned our boutique, we loved attending apparel markets and gift shows in search of new merchandise. Seldom did sales representatives disturb us in our store, saving us from the awkward situation of leaving our customers unattended in order to speak with them.

Later, when I worked as manager of admissions supervising the gate attendants at the Oregon Convention Center, I often strolled through the various trade shows we hosted, marveling at the large variety of vendors and attendees.

Given my prior experience, I felt trade shows might expand our exposure more efficiently to a much larger customer base faster than traveling door to door, espresso bar after coffee house. Instead of being perceived by busy owners or managers as more of a nuisance than as an opportunity, chatting about your business at a trade show was not only welcome - it was expected. That's what everyone was there for.

Everyone on the trade floor was actively seeking innovative new products. They are in the right frame of mind to be receptive to new ideas and merchandise that can either assist them or help them grow their respective businesses. And that's one sole proprietor after another, one distributor after another. You might luck out and have a buyer for a national retail chain stroll into your booth. You just pitch your heart out and collect cards galore to follow-up on for months to come.

Not only is the stream of potential new customers endless, but new suppliers are everywhere. Creative supply and equipment solutions are plentiful and the educational seminars are invaluable. Immersing yourself in a trade show could transform your business.

I was committed to mobilize Oregon Chai for a consistent and all-out trade show campaign. I saw this as a rich and fertile untapped marketing tool but the rest of my team needed convincing. I suggested that we all attend a show, just for a look-see, so they could get a feel for the possibilities.

Lori couldn't miss work at her day job, so the rest of us: Heather, Brian, Carla and I, flew to San Diego for the February 1995 Fancy Food Show presented by the National Association for the Specialty Food Trade.

Since we (always) had limited funds, the four of us shared the same hotel room. Heather and I shared one bed, Carla took the second and poor Brian was banished to the roll-out. It was crowded, but fun. We crawled over beds, stepped over luggage and shimmied around one another. The bathroom, on the other hand, was another story. Getting four people showered and ready each morning with only one sink and one shower was a perpetual study in patience.

When the show opened, Carla and I wandered its aisles together. With vast samples of candies, snacks and gourmet items, we tried everything. It was, after all, a gourmet food show. By noon, we both felt bloated and nauseous from all the delicious, rich foods we had tasted.

"We really ought to try and pace ourselves," I warned Carla, as much a warning to her as a reminder to myself. "We don't want to be sick the entire time."

"Yes," she said, patting her sore stomach. "I know."

But it was so hard to resist. I mean, this was the cream of the crop. So, despite uncomfortable, ever-tightening belts and fatigued feet, we plowed on, eager to see (and taste) everything we could. We chatted with vendors, but called on our deepest reserves of willpower (and sympathy for our gurgling stomachs) to stop sampling every morsel they offered.

We didn't see much of Brian or Heather. We'd separated earlier that morning. They were off exploring on their own, speaking with vendors and absorbing as much information as they could, too. Divide and conquer, that was our strategy.

Amid our strolls, we got the chance to speak with several people about our chai. As we didn't have a booth, it was hard to siphon off potential interest from the middle of aisles but the experience achieved my initial goals: it easily convinced the rest of my team how worthwhile it would be to exhibit in a booth.

We noticed one company selling tea, but no one offered chai.

"That's a good sign," I said, glancing around. "That means the market is wide open."

"Yeah," Carla grinned, "It looks like we've got it all to ourselves."

We needed to figure out a way to capitalize on these kinds of opportunities in the future. We couldn't let a single one slip through our fingertips. Trade shows offered the potential to exponentially skyrocket our schlepping one-on-one taste testing efforts.

That evening, after the San Diego show closed, Carla and I, both painfully bloated, hit the hay while the tireless young ones visited Tijuana. Heather bought and ate food directly from the street vendors. I'd heard about people becoming ill by eating contaminated food in Mexico. It was so like Heather - always taking risks, always up for anything, always having a good time.

After the trade show, we knew we needed to promote Oregon Chai at the next one. But the exhibition fees were prohibitive. And to even get a booth at one of these trade shows, your company had to be a member of the National Association for the Specialty Food Trade - and we couldn't afford that. We needed to figure out a way to have a presence at one of these major trade shows without going broke doing it.

Starbucks called.

They wanted to buy our recipe.

What a thrilling endorsement of our quality and obvious potential!

Lori and Heather met with Starbucks several more times, trying to strike some sort of a distribution deal but Starbucks only wanted to buy our recipe. They didn't want to work with us.

We considered it.

We spoke with our attorney and debated amongst the five of us the best course of action. We finally agreed that twenty-five thousand dollars was a viable sales figure.

On the one hand, that seemed unfathomably exorbitant just for a recipe. On the other hand, it didn't seem to be quite fair for all the groundwork we'd done building the business beyond just the recipe itself - not to mention the impressive, momentum we'd created.

Just the same, we were all tired of working for free and who knew if we'd regret not having grabbed the cash bird in the hand when it presented itself? Would we just continue to plunge money, time and energy down this black hole?

Certainly none of us were going to retire with one-fifth of twenty-five thousand after taxes and attorney's fees. We loved our company. We all really enjoyed our jobs. And we all loved our chai. If we sold our recipe to Starbucks, we simply wouldn't have a business at all any more. After several weeks, we ultimately decided that we all had enough faith in the potential of Oregon Chai to keep going. Tempting as it was, we decided not to sell.

Heather and Lori's repeated meetings with Starbucks had an obvious drawback, a calculated risk we'd agreed to take: we had simply educated our biggest competitor about an entirely new category and whet their appetite to muscle in on our territory.

Little David had inadvertently awakened the sleeping giant Goliath.

We're Hemorrhaging Cash...Show Us the Money, Puhleeze!

As we entered into retail, distribution became increasingly complex. Still, out of the back of my car, I delivered cases of Oregon Chai concentrate to our customer's stores via their rear loading docks. Managers would greet me with label guns. I would dial the expiration date and price and tag each container. When completed, I'd stock the store's refrigerated case with all the containers and put any back stock on a shelf in their inventory coolers.

Some store's refrigerated sections were more difficult to access than others. One in particular, I remember, was only accessible through a large overstocked cooler. When I opened the cooler door, I found it stuffed with boxes. There was nowhere to walk and I wasn't sure what to do. I glanced around for assistance, but found none. I finally decided that, in order to reach the front where I had to stock my product - the refrigerated glass display shelves where grocery shoppers get their dairy products and orange juice - I would have to climb up on top of the boxes and crawl over there.

I set my eighteen-pound case of chai on top of the tower of boxes, grabbed a nearby step stool and summitted the five-foot wall of cardboard. This left only two feet of crawl space above my head. Like a soldier slithering under barbed wire in an enemy's field, I heaved the box of chai, alternately sliding and dragging it alongside me through the cooler's frigid air. Finally, I inched my way to the front of the case. Balancing gingerly atop my precarious perch, I dropped down to the floor and dragged my case one last time, opened it and placed the fresh containers on the shelves. Mission accomplished.

Now the challenge was getting back.

The panic of claustrophobia overcame me as I looked back at the stack of boxes blocking the exit of the cooler. What if I can't get out? What if I get stuck? I imagined shivering to death behind the milk, praying someone would reach in for a gallon of skim milk and see me and scream, alerting the unavailable store's staff to race for help before I died of hypothermia.

As I inched my way back, my mind reeled: Will I be able to open the big cooler door from the inside? Can I even reach the door's handle from up here? What was I thinking? Unlike Carla's I Love Lucy debacle with the conveyor belt just a few months prior, I was spared being locked in a refrigerated case and made it back out with no trouble. What an imagination, I laughed once outside. A friend of mine once said "Tedde, when other people see a barrier they stop, but you see a barrier and just climb over it." If he only knew how true that was.

Each week we held a meeting to check in with one another and keep tabs on how everyone was doing. We set and discussed our goals. During one of these gatherings, we decided we needed a mission statement. So we brainstormed.

"Let's say 'we make the best chai in the world!'" Heather and Brian offered grandiosely.

"That's pretty ambitious,"I said, thinking that was a rather bold statement. "Do we really have to make the best chai in the world? I mean, can't we just make great chai? Why the best in the world?"

As the one responsible for actually making the chai, I thought being the best chai in the world was perhaps asking a tad more than I could personally deliver.

But I was overruled. And our company's mission statement evolved into: "To be the best tasting, highest quality all natural chai in the world; to be the leading brand and the category maker; and to be a successful and socially responsible company that values the environment, community, customers, employees, suppliers as well as shareholders."

Ultimately, along with everyone else on our weary little team, I was inspired and re-energized by our mission statement. I often referred to our Oregon Chai mission statement - especially the part about "making the best chai in the world" to support my decisions, though sometimes at a slightly higher cost, to purchase only the very best ingredients. It also led me to continue to pursue, whenever possible, the use of organic products (those raised without the use of synthetic pesticides or fertilizers). The tea we bought was grown biodynamically (a self-sufficient, lunar-based approach to organic farming) and, whenever we could, we purchased from producers who practiced "Fair Trade" (where the workers are paid at least the nation's minimum wage and are provided with safe, healthy working conditions and opportunities for advancement).

Our decisions paid off.

Oregon Chai grew at a phenomenal rate. It was all each of us could do to keep up. We were having a good time and our spirits remained high. No one worried about the future. We were simply too busy.

We had so much that we needed to do that in order to succeed, there was no way we could make Oregon Chai a true success unless we all committed to working full time. The company needed our full attention.

Heather and Lori each worked additional jobs for survival income. Heather babysat and worked part-time for the recycling program at Portland State University. It seemed she was always weighing garbage or getting on or off a garbage truck. Lori worked full-time for an ad agency and that was always a source of concern for us. Her help was so instrumental, but when could she commit to coming over full-time? Brian scraped by on savings and cut all his expenses to the bone by riding his bike everywhere and, when necessary, driving a used Volkswagen bus. Carla and I were lucky: we had husbands who supported us. And I had the luxury of pursuing my degree, finally. My goal was still to graduate before I hit the half-century mark in the midst of all this.

We paid cash for everything. Initially the money came out of my personal checking account but later, Carla started sharing the burden with me, too. We were able to cover the costs of ingredients and supplies. Still, none of us were earning any money, we weren't even making minimum wage, which, obviously, placed a significant strain on everyone. We couldn't go on like this.

One afternoon, Lori told me she'd had dinner with Heather and some friends the night before. Everyone was having a good time visiting, until the waiter came to take their orders - and the atmosphere suddenly changed.

"Heather started crying," Lori said. "She had no money for her dinner. She's so poor, she couldn't even order coffee and wouldn't ask anyone for help."

I felt horrible. Were we doing the right thing? How could I let my daughter go through this? My heart broke a little that day.

I worried relentlessly about where our company was headed but Heather was resiliently optimistic and had never complained. Just a couple of months earlier, The Daily Journal of Commerce quoted her infectious optimism: "I'm hoping once we start selling enough of it, those nickels and dimes will start adding up."

But I wondered if we'd ever catch up with our own growth. It seemed the more chai we sold, the more we'd need to produce and the increased production costs guzzled up any cash reserves we could manage to save. I spoke with our accountants asking if they could find a way to at least compensate Heather. A few days later, I received this letter:

> Dear Tedde:
>   Enclosed is our analysis of your current operations.
>   If you want to be able to pay Heather $150 per week, you would need to clear at least $780 per month. The current production level only produces $522 of gross profit per month. If the monthly expenses shown here are correct, you need to increase your sales and production to five batches of regular and two batches of decaf per month.

We started paying Heather anyway - one hundred dollars a week - not what I'd hoped, but better than nothing. The rest of us continued to work for free.

With the increase in sales and, consequently, distribution, there just wasn't enough time to do everything necessary to run our start-up company, over-see production and deliver Oregon Chai personally to all of our accounts. We needed distributors. One day, as I stood in front of a refrigerated case filling its shelves with Oregon Chai, I noticed a young fellow placing fresh, bottled juice into the case beside me.

"Are you a distributor?" I asked.

"Yes," he said. "I work for a small, local company."

I was intrigued and thought perhaps he could help us.

"Would you be interested in distributing our product, too?"

He nodded. "Sure, I'll ask my boss," he said.

I jotted down my name and phone number and gave it to him and a day or two later, his employer phoned us.

"We'd be very interested in distributing Oregon Chai," he said. "Can we set up a meeting?"

We met with the owner of the company one evening at Carla's home. He was kind and I soon found that we shared many of the same values: natural foods, good customer service and we both loved Oregon Chai products. The downside was that he asked for an exclusive agreement. This aspect of our relationship would mean that he would enjoy sole distributorship of Oregon Chai products to natural product stores throughout our region. None of us liked that idea. We were concerned that if we signed an exclusive agreement with one company, we may miss an opportunity for a more suitable arrangement later as we learned more about the marketplace.

Considering our rapid growth, forecasting any future growth was difficult. We didn't want Oregon Chai wrapped up in a contract that might inhibit us. But at the time, we couldn't find anyone else willing to help. The other distributors were too large and weren't even interested in speaking with us. We just couldn't continue to deliver Oregon Chai ourselves. Something had to give.

So, more out of desperation than willingness, we agreed to his terms. We signed a contract and he began distribution. I was relieved that I no longer bore that burden. My distribution duties were reduced to making sure there were simply sufficient cases of chai to fulfill his orders. That was a relief.

About a month after signing the agreement with our new distributor, we received a call from another one. The second distributor's client base was unlike our current one. Their territories were not overlapping, which meant that we could employ both without infringing on the exclusive agreement of the first. So we signed on with them as well. We now had two distributors in two different territories. We were growing at light speed.

Just a Couple Thousand Tea Bags

The demand for Oregon Chai was expanding so rapidly, we needed yet another, larger production facility. Brian, now an integral part of our team, spoke with the manager of a new location about producing our chai and the manager agreed. This new facility owned five-hundred-gallon kettles and offered us the capability of filling half-gallon and gallon containers.

Because the facility's equipment was set up for cartons and could not accommodate plastic, we decided to use paper-based cartons, like the ones used for orange juice, rather than the plastic containers we'd been using. Everyone reassured me that the cartons would work fine. I wanted to believe this: they were less expensive, so this seemed like a better solution. At least that's what I wanted to think.

Freud once said: "...nothing is more readily believed than that which meets our own wishes and desires halfway." We believe what we want to believe, what suits our purposes. I should've listened to Freud.

We proceeded to produce our chai concentrate in our new, larger containers while we continued packing our smaller quarts and pints with our original manufacturer. With this new co-packer, we had gotten up to five hundred gallon-sized batches. This was especially hard for me to wrap my mind around as I had been producing what seemed like the monumental eight-gallon batches just months ago.

Everyone at the new plant worked hard for us and they were always cheerful. It was an ideal relationship. We used our handmade bridal-fabric teabags to hold the tea and spices for steeping. The guys at the plant thought we were using pantyhose because they had been stained brown from all the tea. In retrospect, I thought, why didn't we just use pantyhose? A ninety-nine cent solution. Sheesh.

In order to squeeze every ounce of flavor from the teabags, I purchased a metal, industrial-sized floor-mop wringer. This did a fairly good job of pressing all the flavored liquid out of the hot, wet bags steaming with rich ingredients. Still, the wringer was awkward and heavy and required workers to heave it over their shoulders and up onto the edge of the massive, hot kettles. In the back of my mind, I feared that in my absence, someone might find the wringer in a storage closet and decide it would work great for wringing out a dirty mop. As far as I know, that never happened. I hope.

In less than a year, we'd outgrown Heather's bedroom. In April of 1995, Brian found us an office by peddling his bike around the reduced-rent district on the east side of the Willamette River in southeast Portland. It was ideal: centrally located, easy and convenient for everyone. Both the freeway and the bridge leading to most of our homes were nearby. We could walk downtown or catch the corner bus and the rent was reasonable.

The building on South East Ninth Street wasn't elaborate but it suited our needs. There was a large room with two desks and a conference table and three small offices with a bit of warehouse space. A year later, INC Magazine's article would describe it perfectly: "the 1,056-square-foot headquarters is dingy, but at $885 per month, the price is right." While our office was indeed "dingy," it was clean. Still, the surrounding neighborhood was what some might call "colorful." One day, I discovered a used syringe on the windowsill outside. And our local newspaper reported a shooting at a bowling alley just down the street. Heather had her purse stolen right out from her desk, but other than that, we never had any other trouble.

Our most challenging issue was parking. The spaces surrounding our building were all zoned two-hour parking. I phoned the traffic management department of the Portland Department of Transportation, hoping for some compassion.

"Can't you change the parking restrictions?" I asked. "The two-hour limits just aren't enough time for the people who work in this area."

"Your landlord must sign a letter requesting the change," the city rep told me.

Our landlord was happy to help and the two-hour limitation was soon eliminated. But in the end, it didn't end up helping us at all because commuters discovered this free all day parking haven and began parking their vehicles right outside our building and walking across the bridge to their downtown jobs. I learned quickly just why the two-hour limit had been established.

Given the dogged determination apparently ingrained in my family, I didn't give up. I put fliers under the windshield wipers of commuters' cars that read: "HELP! The parking in this area is extremely limited. Please park as close as you can to the vehicle in front of or behind you so we can all park. Thank you."

It didn't do any good.

Drivers continued parking their cars at least a half car length either from the corner or from the vehicle in front of them. I finally relented and simply endured the situation like everyone else.

Shortly after we'd set up office, Brian finished our business plan and used it to apply for a $50,000 Small Business Administration loan. He met regularly with the manager of Pacific One Bank, arriving nearly every day astride his well-worn bicycle.

When he first met Brian, the manager didn't take him seriously. Brian dressed casually, his hair in its usual ponytail, carrying a well-worn backpack. But, like the rest of us, Brian was nothing if not persistent - and his persistence paid off. After many trips with the tires on his bike wearing thin, the bank finally conceded to process our loan request - but there was a catch: the bank would only approve the loan if we used my house as collateral.

With my lack of experience, I hadn't realized that placing a lien on my home would be a requirement. But my husband agreed to put our family home on the line with me.

"I know it's a big risk," he said, "but I am amazed at the way your product can convert the disinterested."

Without complaint, my husband agreed to offer up our family home as collateral for the business line of credit - but on one condition: I must be named the Chairman of the Board of Directors until the loan was paid in full and the lien released. So, we submitted the loan application - and prayed for a desperately needed loan approval.

Heather was forever figuring out ways to be of service to our customers and raise awareness about the product she loved so much.

One morning, between 1 and 5 AM, Heather provided chai samples to the drivers of one of our distributors before they all left for their various truck routes. She showed the drivers how the chai should be prepared and helped them wake up to steaming, before-the-crack-of-dawn samples.

As they sipped, Heather answered questions and explained our marketing program. By tasting it themselves, the drivers now knew what was in the back of their trucks, what this chai cargo actually was, how it was prepared and how it should taste. Even at one in the morning, we managed to convert a few bleary-eyed truck drivers.

In March, Portland State University's weekly newspaper, The Daily Vanguard, published the first picture featuring our newest, vegan, Zen-studying partner, Brian. The paper stated that I had grown tired of Heather complaining "for the hundredth time about wanting to start her own business." I found it an interesting comment, since Heather never complained. It was simply not part of her nature - at least not any part I'd ever known. I shared the article with Heather.

"Where do these journalists get their information?" Heather asked after reading it.

"I have no idea," I said. "Certainly not from me!"

Even though this particular article proved to be the most exaggerated of any I'd read, we were still grateful for the publicity.

One morning, at the plant as we were preparing to brew, I noticed our tea was missing. Oh, no, I thought, our tea was locked up in Heather's car parked in front of her house. And none of us had keys. Worst of all - Heather was out-of-state in Seattle. She was meeting with the intractable Starbucks representatives, still trying to convince them to distribute our product.

I panicked. I wasn't thinking clearly. Maybe it was a menopausal brain fart but instead of simply calling a locksmith, I raced to the store and purchased several dozen boxes of tea. When I opened the boxes, to my utter dismay, I discovered that rather than the bulk tea I thought I'd bought, I'd grabbed boxes filled with a hundred traditional tea bags - each individually wrapped in those tiny little white envelopes. What was I thinking? I was certain I was losing my mind.

But I had no time to dwell on my stupidity. The water was already boiling in the kettles - and we were on the clock. The co-packer's entire production staff was waiting on me to provide them the ingredients to start brewing. I had no choice.

Humiliated, I brought in all of the boxes of wrapper-encased tea. Everyone else knew instantly what a bonehead maneuver I'd made but the crew was nothing but patient. If they were justifiably laughing at me, they never revealed it.

I was handed a large trashcan for the boxes and wrappers and descended with my tail between my legs down into the basement to unwrap the couple thousand teabags all by my lonesome. I felt terrible and kept beating myself up for creating an even direr situation. Well, I thought, nothing to it but to do it.

I sliced open each box, ripped the paper envelopes off each and every tea bag and piled them up. It was nightmarish. I couldn't work fast enough. One of the production supervisors came down and silently began unwrapping tea bags alongside me. I didn't know what to say to him. I couldn't even make eye contact with him to thank him, I was so mortified. I just kept my head ashamedly bowed and ripped off wrappers as quickly as my hands would allow.

Because of my mistake, we didn't produce as much chai that day as we'd planned. But the entire staff and management never batted an eye and never mentioned the incident again. From that day on, I made certain I had plenty of ingredients in stock far ahead of production time.

"I just spoke with Ben Cohen," Heather said as she popped her head into my office.

"Who's Ben Cohen?" I asked. The name sounded familiar, but I couldn't quite place it.

"Oh mom, you know, of Ben and Jerry's," she said. "The ice cream?"

I was astonished and proud. She'd just up and cold called one of the most well-established, famous business people in our country. I would never have had the courage, but Heather was always courageous. (Just good genes, I guess.)

"It's no big deal," she said. "I just thought I'd ask if he had any advice for our new company."

I grinned. She thought nothing of it. For Heather, it was just another day in the office, finding solutions to everyday dilemmas. It was the principal reason our company had achieved any success at all: we knew what we didn't know - and we weren't afraid to ask for help.

Crying Over Sour Grapes

In the spring of 1995, when we first began discussing our need for new marketing materials, Heather believed we needed a fresh, improved appearance. We agreed to hire a professional design firm, so Brian and Heather began a search. It was our communal understanding that the two of them would speak with three or four agencies, collect all their proposals, and present them to the rest of us. As a group, we would agree on the one we liked best.

Back on the production front, our new production facility began noticing rings from the chai on the sides of the stainless steel kettles. They had a hard time scouring them off and the Quality Control Manager was concerned that the stains might contaminate other products. Our own worries never made it that far.

A young woman called my office and said: "Your chai tastes like dirt."

I chatted with her briefly but dismissed her concerns: you either loved Oregon Chai or you hated it. There was rarely any in between. The response to Oregon Chai was seldom lukewarm. She probably just doesn't like it, I thought. I ignored her remark and forgot about her call.

The next day, our distributor called.

"I need to meet with you and Heather immediately," he said. "We have a problem."

Heather and I jumped in the car and drove to his office, concerned. When we arrived, we were escorted through an immense warehouse filled with the scent of coffee. There were lots of people packing and preparing boxes for shipping. At the very rear of the warehouse, we entered a corridor that lead to a large conference room.

It was quiet, considerably different than the busy warehouse we'd just hiked through. The owner entered with his public relations director and a young woman. On the table in front of us sat two half-gallon cartons of Oregon Chai.

"Take a look at these," the owner said, angrily.

Heather and I each opened a container and gasped. Not only did they smell rancid, but there was an enormous, yellowy-orange mass floating on top resembling a huge sea sponge. I felt an immediate wrench in my stomach and worried I'd puke.

"I'm the one who called you about the dirty chai," the young woman said.

I was mortified. I had a sinking feeling that I had not given her call the weight it obviously deserved.

"After calling you about the off-flavor, I opened a container and this is what I found," she explained.

I was humiliated, embarrassed.

"What are you going to do?" asked the owner.

I was confused. I didn't know what to say. I had no idea what the problem was much less the remedy.

I looked at Heather.

Heather looked at me.

We both just stared at the table.

"I think what we're seeing is mold," he said. "My wife is allergic to it."

Mold, I thought, how could mold get into our chai?

"I'm so sorry," I said. "We will get this straightened out right away."

We left the conference room. As I strode through the vast warehouse, I just knew everyone was leering at me, disgusted, knowing I was the one responsible for this foul situation. I wished I were invisible. It seemed like miles from the conference room at the back of the warehouse to the front door where we'd come in - I thought we'd never reach it.

We recalled all of the containers. It was necessary to act quickly to retrieve as much of the questionable product as possible before any more customers discovered the mold. But how would we find it all? And how would we retrieve it?

Luckily, we were still a small company and didn't have a huge customer base. But what about the cost? This mistake would surely cost us much more than any of our previous mishaps. Could we pull the funds together? What about our reputation? Could we bounce back from this? Would our customers still trust us? Would they still purchase and drink Oregon Chai? The questions came so quickly, my mind was a jumbled mass.

I hurried samples of the tainted chai over to the lab, trying to figure out what on earth had gone wrong this time. They ran a number of tests and found that our distributor was right: the product did indeed contain mold. It was a common and non-toxic type, thankfully, but mold nonetheless. So the five of us - Carla, Heather, Lori, Brian and I - gathered and decided on a plan of attack.

Carla pulled every purchase order and began calling our customers to locate all of the moldy chai. Our manufacturers also needed to be notified. Brian spoke with the owner of the production plant while I talked with their Quality Control Manager.

"I thought this would happen," he said.

"What!?" I wanted to scream at him: "Why didn't you say something earlier? This recall is going to set us back about fourteen thousand dollars!" But I didn't say any of that - it was too late - what we needed now was a solution. We needed to move forward, rationally. We had to remove the affected product from the shelves immediately - and establish mold prevention strategies for the future.

There's always a tendency to want to blame someone or something. My partners suggested that it was the fault of the production facility: it probably wasn't as clean as it should have been, they suggested. Or maybe the mold grew because the containers were dusty? But there are mold spores in the air everywhere. All the time.

It turned out to be the "fault" of the cartons. According to a microbiologist I consulted with, the paper cartons were just a bad idea from the start. Freud was right: we had brushed our legitimate concerns under the rug in honor of the path of least resistance, the easiest route. A perishable product cannot be placed in a container that is not sterilized and tightly sealed. As long as oxygen can get into the container, mold spores can sneak in, too.

It was no one's fault.

It was everyone's fault.

It was a time for more deep breaths.

Stop whining, I told myself, clean up this mess and get on with your business.

We started the recall using our own cars for product retrieval. Luckily for us, our customers understood. In just two long days, we rounded up all the carton-packed chai. What to do with them was our next hurdle.

We were unsure how many of the cases packed in our cars were spoiled - or how many might spoil in the future. Worse yet, the county dump refused to take the chai. They said they didn't know what it was and therefore weren't sure if it could go in the dump. But they agreed to take the empty cartons.

So, just like our honey disaster all over again, we enlisted the help of family and friends. But this was a five hundred gallon batch as opposed to the hundred and eighty-five gallon batch we'd had to destroy because of the inexpensive baker's honey.

Still, we were fortunate. Scores of people showed up, including my two teenage nephews. Bless their energy and willingness to do the tough jobs. Hard-working and with attitudes to match, they stood in the bathrooms, opened containers and poured the contents into the awaiting toilets. Others dumped chai down drain holes in the warehouse's floor. The empty containers were crushed and tossed into a box. These were then carried outside and flung into a drop box.

We were like a swarm of worker bees from whence our chai came. We cleaned up our home and made it usable again.

I tasted the suspect chai. I wanted to know if it really would make anyone sick - and if so, it might as well be me. Menopausal thinking doesn't always make sense.

Finally, after hours of labor, we took a well-deserved break. We ordered a ton of pizzas for our hungry crew. The atmosphere was like a party. After several more hours, the drop box was stuffed to its brim.

Next, came the warehouse's gummy, chai-encrusted floor. We all grabbed mops and dove in. We mopped and wiped, cleaned and scrubbed. And though we swabbed it several times, the floor remained sticky and stayed so for many weeks. I deemed it a gentle reminder for a more promising future.

Speaking of future, our bank called. Our loan was finally approved! And could my husband and I come in today to sign the loan documents? I looked over at David and down at my chai-soaked clothes. Both exhausted from hours of dumping suspect chai, we ran home to clean up and change into something that looked a little more professional, responsible and credible.

We arrived at the bank and were seated at a large, rectangular table. To calm myself as we waited, I meditated on the pair of long, slender, ceremonial-looking pens, standing at attention in their marble, gilt-edged holder next to our pile of loan documents.

I chatted with the escrow officer and prayed I wouldn't have to lie. I didn't want any questions that would result in my telling them that we were in the midst of a recall. I was afraid that if they found out, our loan would fall apart - along with our business. I felt I'd implode with the stress. My knees knocked together, my voice shook, my stomach churned.

I felt nauseated and wondered if it was from sipping the moldy tea (whose idea was that?!) or just a case of overworked nerves. After what seemed like hours and signing what felt like an acre of financial paperwork, we finally reached the last signature line on the last sheet. We had reached the bottom of the pile without any leak of our recall or any probing into our firm's condition, today.

The funds were transferred into our depleted account - saving our company from certain failure - and my stomach finally settled. The tea hadn't made me sick after all - and I took that as an omen that Oregon Chai would survive.

Even though our loan was approved, the chai recall kissed goodbye any hopes we had of salaries looming on our horizon. Getting paid was a moot point anyway because before the ink was even dry on the loan papers secured by a lien on my home, Heather and Brian returned excited from a meeting at the ad agency where Lori worked and instead of presenting us with a proposal - Brian and Heather proudly handed us a signed contract - attached to a fifty thousand dollar price tag - that they had already committed to, just the two of them.

I was speechless. I could barely breathe. All fifty thousand. Poof! Just like that. With the snap of fingers, the swoop of one signature. When we had so many other urgent needs simultaneously demanding the funds - how could they?

"How could you make this kind of commitment without consulting the rest of us?" I asked, enraged. "We're supposed to be a team and this isn't how teams work!"

I was flabbergasted. I just stood there, my mouth agape, staring at the two of them.

I looked over at Carla, who was sheet white. Up until this point, Carla and I had been subsidizing the company. Typically, Carla maintained a jubilant sense of humor. But she looked as if every ounce of blood had just drizzled from her body. She looked numb.

"I have deliveries to make several miles outside of Portland," she said, barely. "I have to leave." And she limped out of the room.

Carla told me later that she was so distressed that she steered to the side of the road, opened her car door - and vomited. That was certainly how I felt.

After Carla left, I stood there, staring at Heather and Brian, anger oozing. I was livid. I lost control.

"I've got to go!" I shouted and left the room.

My emotions were out of control and I had to do something about it. I just couldn't take this kind of stress any more. I phoned my doctor and made an emergency appointment for the following morning. During our visit, after discussing my extreme prolonged stress at length, my physician prescribed Paxil.

Ironically, at precisely the same time I was imploding, Heather was quoted in an article about working alongside her mother: "It works," she said. "Because if your mom gets mad at you, it doesn't matter because it's just your mom."

I smiled, pissed off. It was complicated. I was simultaneously proud of her for being such an audacious risk taker - and livid that she was doing so with my assets! I trusted her instincts but I just didn't share her sense of adventure because she wasn't old enough to share my appreciation for security, for what my husband and I had worked so hard to provide - for her. She took it for granted and yet capitalized on it. And what had it all been for all along if not to give our children a better life? A strong footing? Like I said, it was complicated.

She's right, I thought as I read the article. No matter how much we disagree, I will always be her mother - and I will always love her.

I took some Paxil, downed it with some chai and headed back to work.

A few days later, Carla and I went back to our distributor's warehouse where the mold had first been discovered. Twelve pallets - about nine hundred remaining cases of chai - sat waiting to be destroyed.

The two of us would have to dump all the rest by ourselves. The distributor told us that a couple of men would assist us but all they did was give us containers for the emptied cartons - and then disappeared.

I opened one carton and gagged at the sight of a mass of lengthy, jet-black, slimy material and its pungent odor. All in all, though, less than a handful of cartons had large, visible chunks of mold.

As Carla and I examined the other containers of chai, we noticed that some of the plastic pints and quarts had bits of mold floating in them, too. How could that have happened? This problem was supposed to have stemmed from the new paper cartons. What was going on now?

We'd had the chai tested for shelf stability and there was no microbial growth in containers held at room temperature for several months. The mold should only have been in the new packaging. What was suddenly wrong with the plastic containers we'd been using all along? I was baffled.

After speaking with the manufacturer and witnessing their procedures, I noted that the bottles were filled faster than the workers could cap them. As had become our production method, the containers were filled automatically - but the bottles were still capped by hand. Filled bottles would stand on a table while a worker screwed on their lids. Sometimes the bottles were so numerous that the worker couldn't seal them quickly enough. Consequently, some would have time to cool. I theorized that the mold spores infected the plastic containers because the bottles were allowed to cool before they were capped. Mold spores could easily survive at these cooler temperatures. And if they weren't destroyed initially, they then had the perfect environment for growth.

A day or two later, we received a call from the food lab technician who had recommended that we use fruit juice in our concentrate to lower its pH.

"I found some information about the white grape juice you're using," she said. "It contains a mold spore that's resistant to high temperatures."

WHAT?

"I thought it was supposed to make the product better, not worse," I responded.

The grape juice was the last thing we had added to the chai - and we hadn't performed shelf-life studies on the concentrate with the grape juice after its addition. It just never occurred to me that this change could make a difference. The brew was pasteurized before being bottled, but apparently even that temperature was not high enough to eradicate this spore.

Once again, I felt dizzy and nauseous. How could so many things go wrong? How many more lessons can I endure?

With mold inhabiting the plastic containers, too, yet another recall was necessary. Not to mention, a third round of dumping. Would this ever end? Or would it be the end of us first?

At least this time, there weren't as many containers. Another blessed nephew came to our rescue. He loaded the bottles into the bed of his pickup truck then dumped them into a local landfill. None of us said anything and I was relieved to have this episode finally behind me.

Following this most recent incident, Carla sat down with our accountants. We needed to figure out exactly how much money we'd lost and how we should proceed.

At the time, Carla's daughter attended Oregon State University. On one of her trips visiting her daughter at OSU, Carla learned about their Food Science Department. She spoke with the head of its food sensory division.

"We have a program at OSU that might interest you," she said. "We have an advisory team that will meet with you for a nominal fee and help with any aspect of your business."

We set up a meeting immediately. Heather, Brian, Carla and I met with their advisors. We told them every detail of the problems we had experienced. We sought advice on ways to improve our packaging and manufacturing processes.

"Microorganisms need certain conditions in which to thrive," the team's microbiologist explained. "You need to analyze your product to see what conditions are required to make it safe. Then you must establish barriers that will prevent organisms from growing. Obviously, the pH is critical but the temperature at which the product is packed and stored - and, of course, the packaging itself - are all critical elements as well."

"Everything pretty much revolves around the pH of the product," he continued, "high or low - even if the pH is low, below 4.5, you may need to add some type of acid to keep it safe. Once you know the pH, you need to process your product accordingly and pick the packaging best suited for its storage and use."

I thought about what he was telling us. Our product was acidic, which made handling easier than a lower-acid product, like milk.

"Botulism won't grow in an acidic environment," he continued. "However, yeast and mold will. To kill the yeast and mold spores, you need heat and packaging that's impervious to air."

I knew it. The cartons were simply a horrible idea from the start. Our plastic containers worked fine as long as we sealed them while the chai was still hot. If the lids were put on after it had cooled, spores were likely present inside the lids, which would then grow after we affixed them.

"Finally," he said, "unless it's been aseptically packaged, the chai needs to be stored at temperatures below forty-five degrees Fahrenheit."

We thanked him for his time and input. I had no idea what on earth an "aseptic" package was. I researched it immediately and learned that it was a container that is sterilized before filling and can hold food products at room temperature. It's what is typically used for soy and rice milk. That sounded like a reasonable solution but we couldn't afford to change everything over at the moment. I wished I had learned about it earlier - but I was happy to have the information now for our move-forward strategies.

Heather and Lori worked on mending our strained customer relationships and salvaging our bruised reputation. They penned the following letter:

May 23, 1995

Dear Customer,

We want to thank you for all of your support during our first year of business. Thus far, 1995 has been a challenging and exciting time for Oregon Chai. During the past month, we have experienced some changes we want to share with you.

Through careful, methodical testing last fall, Oregon Chai was shown by our food lab to have a seven-month shelf life while refrigerated and a four-month shelf life at room temperature. In order for us to store and ship our product at room temperature, the State of Oregon, Department of Agriculture, Food Safety Division, required that the pH for the chai be lowered to below 4.2. This was accomplished with the addition of white grape juice concentrate.

Unfortunately, this did not work and we found mold in a few of the containers that had been held at room temperature, i.e. out of 135 half-gallons of original recipe in cartons, we found 9 with mold.

Because of our commitment to quality, we pulled all product that had the possibility of becoming contaminated. We then began an investigation into the source and a solution to the problem. We have met with specialists of the Food Sciences Department at Oregon State University and they made some suggestions as to how we can assure the quality and shelf life of Oregon Chai.

The product must be refrigerated. We have been assured by all the "experts" that refrigeration will "retard" the growth of yeasts and molds – just like any other fresh food product in your refrigerator. Consequently, we now store our product at a cold-storage facility. All product that is shipped will now be packed with dry ice.

The product's turnover needs to increase. The quicker the Chai is used, the better. This is easy because Oregon Chai is so good no one can keep it in their refrigerator for very long, anyway. Therefore, to insure the rapid turnover of product, Oregon Chai has had to focus on our best sellers - ORIGINAL and DECAF concentrates. We want to guarantee that we provide you with the freshest product. Unfortunately, this means we can no longer produce the less-sweet versions of the product because they simply do not sell as well.

According to the experts, the chai concentrate can only be packaged in glass or plastic. The paper cartons we used were a possible source of contamination.

Remember, Oregon Chai is an all natural food product. As such, it must be treated as any food product: carefully.

Oregon Chai is committed to quality. We will continue to offer you only the very best product available. We love our chai and believe we can provide you with good service and a wonderful, delicious product.

Again, we thank you for your continued support.

Sincerely,
Heather, Tedde, Lori, Carla, Brian

TONIC Jan 18, 1995

← chatter chatter chatter →

SCENE 'N' HERD

Escape artist Reverend Chumleigh couldn't free himself from bureaucratic red tape on Saturday, January 14. The demented daredevil was preparing a Houdini-esque feat that would have had him handcuffed inside of a box and lowered by crane into the chilly Willamette River, but the necessary permits didn't come through. Chumleigh continues to perform his popular vaudeville show at Imago Theater.

Intrepid Hazel/Team Dresch drummer Jody Bleyle was seen causing a minor ruckus Thursday, January 5, passionately tearing down flyers that she deemed pro-rape at Satyricon. The object of her ire? A particular placard for Eric's Punk Rock Show, which featured an armless woman wearing underwear with the words "fuck me" written on them. Bleyle will, aptly enough, appear as a superhero in the new Hazel video, which the band is currently filming.

Now there's a café in town where you can *really* get wired. It's called The Habit, and it sports a bank of computers where you can get 20 minutes of on-line time free with a cup of coffee, or for three bucks an hour. The Habit, which also features a collection of hard-to-find magazines and periodicals, is located at 2633 Southeast 21st at Clinton. For a virtual cup of joe, their E-Mail address is: cafe@habit.com.

A nude photo of MTV VJ Kennedy that had been uploaded onto the internet had ended up in the January issue of Esquire. The photo, taken backstage at a Lollapalooza show, proves that the obnoxious conservative's on-screen personality is not the only thing about her that falls flat. Also included in the issue is a Portland restaurant guide, which includes reviews of Wildwood, Zéfiro, Pazzo Ristorante and the Heathman Hotel.

Oregon Chai-heads Lori Spencer and Heather McMillen, chai-ing one on at The Green Room.

By Dale E. Basye

CHAI: A NEW BREW WITH AN ATTITUDE

Oregon Chai is:
A) a dangerous new martial arts academy that *Willamette Week* is currently investigating.
B) a Tantric sexual position involving twine, pulleys and Oregon Lottery "Scratch-Its."
C) an endangered bird currently giving Oregon's loggers a big headache.
D) dyslexic for "Oregon Chia."
E) a spicy new tea beverage that tastes something like a pumpkin pie latte.

OK, time's up. Pencils down. If you answered anything but "E" you should really up your dosage. But don't despair) Oregon Chai has only been available for a few months, yet is already doing brisk business in nearly 80 coffee shops, restaurants and grocery stores in the greater Portland area.

The idea for Oregon Chai originated when Portlander Heather McMillen, while experiencing massive hair withdrawal during a trek through the Himalayas, ran into an Indian villager, apologized and sampled his aromatic concoction of tea, milk and spices, which he called chai.

Upon McMillen's return to the States, she had friend Lori Spencer sample her version of the tangy elixir, after which Spencer enthusiastically replied, "We have to market this!"

The two of them started producing the buzz-inducing liquid in May in a Methodist church, yet demand quickly necessitated moving manufacturing to Fire Mountain in Clackamas, as well as the enlistment of two more partners, Karla Powell and McMillen's mom Tedda.

Oregon Chai can be served hot or cold, yet enterprising locals are putting their own spin on the drink; Zefiro's features an alcoholic version mixed with brandy and Frangelico called "Fran-Chai," while Crossroads Café adds shots of espresso, resulting in "Death Chai." Future plans include selling it pre-mixed in recyclable cardboard boxes, and perhaps even a Ben & Jerry's Chai ice cream.

"We have teens hooked, as well as people in rest homes," says the animated Spencer of Chai's universal appeal. "While some men initially find it too exotic, women seem to love it so much that they want to bathe in it!"

Oregon Chai can be found at Boyd's Coffee, Umbra Penumbra, The Green Room, Nature's, Marsee Bakery and at Coffee People's airport branch. What you do with it is your business.

Article in the Tonic, 1995

Oregon Chai's first corporate headquarters, 1995

Heather working in the office, 1995

A barista in Portland, Oregon preparing Oregon Chai, 1995

NEWS RELEASE

FOR IMMEDIATE RELEASE

October 31, 1994

FOR MORE INFORMATION
CONTACT:
Heather McMillen (503) 292-6504

OLD WORLD CHAI TO SPICE UP YOUR DAY

"Oregon Chai" Offers An Alternative to Coffee

(Portland, OR) "Oregon Chai", a drink that includes the flavors of black tea, exotic spices, vanilla and sweet honey, is now being offered to coffee shops, stores and restaurants in the Portland Metropolitan area.

Chai, a generic term for tea, is found in India, the Far East, Middle East and Africa, where it is blended with milk and honey.

A versatile beverage, "Oregon Chai" can be served hot (steamed) or cold. "Oregon Chai" is being developed in a market and territory where people are quickly responding. "If people love lattes and espresso drinks , they will love "Oregon Chai," says Heather McMillen, President of "Oregon Chai." "Northwest consumer response so far has been great."

Headquartered in Portland, "Oregon Chai" can be found at Nature's Fresh Northwest, various coffee shops and coffee carts as well as resturants in the greater Portland area.

For further information or a free sampling, please contact Heather or Tedde McMillen at Oregon Chai (503) 292-6504.

###

Oregon Chai's first news release, 1994

Coffee, tea or ... chai?

Non-coffee drink from Himalayas finds acceptance in java-jangled Northwest

By KIM BEELER GOETZ
Daily Journal of Commerce

It's a cross between tea and a latte, and it tastes like a spicy pumpkin pie with egg nog. It's called chai, and it's a tea drink that could take a spot next to coffee in the java-jangled Pacific Northwest.

> *"I think people will like it as much as I do. I'm hoping once we start selling enough of it, those nickels and dimes will start adding up."*
> — Heather McMillen, Oregon Chai

Portlander Heather McMillen found the drink while traveling in the Himalayan Mountains of India. In desperate need of a latte, McMillen said she discovered that Asia had a special drink of its own, known as chai.

After a few swigs of the spicy, sweet beverage, McMillen was hooked, and she hopes Oregonians soon will be hooked, too.

It was after returning to the United States

See CHAI, Page 20

Portlander Heather McMillen samples her Oregon Chai drink under the canopy at Food Front in Northwest Portland. The Himalayan tea drink is gaining popularity in the Northwest.

Greg Paul

that McMillen realized that very few places knew of, let alone served, chai. About a year ago, she decided to make her own brew — Oregon Chai.

McMillen said her formula is similar to the age-old recipe. She added, however, a few ingredients of her own to spice it up — so to speak.

"I'm a vanilla lover," McMillen admitted, and Oregon Chai shows it. The secret concoction includes black tea, honey, vanilla bean and a "potpourri" of natural spices blended with milk. It's served with all varieties of milk, from whole to soy, and is available with or without caffeine.

"If you're a person who has a sweet tooth, Oregon Chai is addicting," McMillen said.

The hot or cold beverage is versatile. It is available in 16-ounce containers from concentrate or by the glass. By next November, McMillen hopes to offer it pre-packaged in milk aseptic bags.

McMillen and her four partners — her mother, Tedde McMillen, and friends Lori Spencer and Carla Powell — may have become a hot investment prospect. Chai is catching on fast in Portland's coffee shops and carts. Oregon Chai is being served throughout metropolitan Portland at such places as Food Front Cooperative Grocery in Northwest Portland, Nature's Fresh Northwest, Besaw's Cafe, Broadway Bakery, Al Volo Coffee Cart at Lamb's Thriftway in Mountain Park, Meetro at Portland State University and Utopia, Dessert and Coffee House.

Specialty coffee roasters/retailers Starbuck's Corp. and Coffee People also are on her list of contacts.

B.R. Schriner, who operates Upfront Caffe at Food Front, said most customers react positively to the drink. In fact, Schriner said a friend with an ulcer tried it, went inside the store to shop, and came out feeling great.

"People love it," Schriner said.

Schriner sells chai drinks for about $2. She also will add a shot of espresso for another 40 cents.

McMillen, a student at Portland State University, said Oregon Chai's production rate is 70 gallons a week, which is expected to soon expand to 200 gallons.

To reach that goal, Oregon Chai is moving its brewing pot out of the kitchen and into Janet Bush's manufacturing business — Fire Mountain in Clackamas. Another small business, Gambee Designs, is doing labeling work as part of a cooperative effort.

Although chai is gaining acceptance, McMillen said there isn't much money coming in. Like most start-up businesses, Oregon Chai has been slow out of the earnings block. However, McMillen is optimistic about the company and its potential.

"I think people will like it as much as I do," she said. "I'm hoping once we start selling enough of it, those nickels and dimes will start adding up."

Vol. 188, No. 49

Daily Journal of Commerce

Portland, Oregon

Tuesday, Nov. 8, 1994

■ The recipe for perpetual igno-rance.
Page 2

DESIGN:
You might like what you see in funds. Page 19.

DONOGHUE:
Doctor earns Kidney Foundation award. Page 4.

NORTHWEST:
Key Bank receives outstanding rating. Page 2.

Article in Daily Journal of Commerce, 1994

SCHEDULE C
(Form 1040)

Department of the Treasury
Internal Revenue Service (U)

Profit or Loss From Business
(Sole Proprietorship)

▶ Partnerships, joint ventures, etc., must file Form 1065.
▶ Attach to Form 1040 or Form 1041. ▶ See Instructions for Schedule C (Form 1040).

OMB No. 1545-0074

1994

Attachment
Sequence No. 09

Name of proprietor *Theodora Jo McMillen*

Social security number (SSN)

A Principal business or profession, including product or service (see page C-1) *Manufacturing - beverage*

B Enter principal business code
(see page C-6) ▶ 1 0 6 3 8

C Business name. If no separate business name, leave blank. *Oregon CHAI (for April - Oct 1, 1994)*

D Employer ID number (EIN), if any

E Business address (including suite or room no.) ▶
City, town or post office, state, and ZIP code *Portland, OR 97521*

F Accounting method: (1) ☒ Cash (2) ☐ Accrual (3) ☐ Other (specify) ▶

G Method(s) used to value closing inventory: (1) ☒ Cost (2) ☐ Lower of cost or market (3) ☐ Other (attach explanation) (4) ☐ Does not apply (if checked, skip line H)   Yes No

H Was there any change in determining quantities, costs, or valuations between opening and closing inventory? If "Yes," attach explanation . . . .   ☒

I Did you "materially participate" in the operation of this business during 1994? If "No," see page C-2 for limit on losses. . .   ☒

J If you started or acquired this business during 1994, check here . . . . ▶ ☒

Part I Income

1 Gross receipts or sales. Caution: If this income was reported to you on Form W-2 and the "Statutory employee" box on that form was checked, see page C-2 and check here . . . . . . ▶ ☐	1	240	45
2 Returns and allowances	2		
3 Subtract line 2 from line 1	3	240	45
4 Cost of goods sold (from line 40 on page 2)	4		
5 Gross profit. Subtract line 4 from line 3	5		
6 Other income, including Federal and state gasoline or fuel tax credit or refund (see page C-2) . . .	6		
7 Gross income. Add lines 5 and 6 . . . . ▶	7	240	45

Part II Expenses. Enter expenses for business use of your home **only** on line 30.

8 Advertising	8	75	84	19 Pension and profit-sharing plans	19			
9 Bad debts from sales or services (see page C-3) . .	9			20 Rent or lease (see page C-4):				
				a Vehicles, machinery, and equipment .	20a	500	—
10 Car and truck expenses (see page C-3)	10	151	67	b Other business property .	20b		
11 Commissions and fees. . .	11			21 Repairs and maintenance . .	21		
12 Depletion.	12			22 Supplies (not included in Part III) .	22	956	09
13 Depreciation and section 179 expense deduction (not included in Part III) (see page C-3) . .	13			23 Taxes and licenses	23		
				24 Travel, meals, and entertainment:			
14 Employee benefit programs (other than on line 19) . . .	14			a Travel	24a		
15 Insurance (other than health) .	15	238	—	b Meals and entertainment .		158	66
16 Interest:				c Enter 50% of line 24b subject to limitations (see page C-4) .		79	35
a Mortgage (paid to banks, etc.) .	16a			d Subtract line 24c from line 24b .	24d	79	33
b Other	16b			25 Utilities	25	142	05
17 Legal and professional services	17	295	—	26 Wages (less employment credits) .	26		
18 Office expense	18			27 Other expenses (from line 46 on page 2)	27		
28 Total expenses before expenses for business use of home. Add lines 8 through 27 in columns. . ▶					28	2437	98
29 Tentative profit (loss). Subtract line 28 from line 7 . . . . *LOSS*					29	(−2233	68)
30 Expenses for business use of your home. Attach Form 8829					30	1205	58
31 Net profit or (loss). Subtract line 30 from line 29.							
• If a profit, enter on Form 1040, line 12, and ALSO on Schedule SE, line 2 (statutory employees, see page C-5). Estates and trusts, enter on Form 1041, line 3.					31	(−3439	26)
• If a loss, you MUST go on to line 32.							

32 If you have a loss, check the box that describes your investment in this activity (see page C-5).
• If you checked 32a, enter the loss on Form 1040, line 12, and ALSO on Schedule SE, line 2 (statutory employees, see page C-5). Estates and trusts, enter on Form 1041, line 3.
• If you checked 32b, you MUST attach Form 6198.

32a ☒ All investment is at risk.
32b ☐ Some investment is not at risk.

For Paperwork Reduction Act Notice, see Form 1040 instructions.   Cat. No. 11334P   Schedule C (Form 1040) 1994

Oregon Chai's 1994 Schedule C

SECTION III:

Let Steep

Sip Quietly and Enjoy

After a month or so, I started tasting an off-flavor in the half-gallon plastic containers. It was not present in the quarts or pints bottled from the same batch and I had never noticed this off-taste in the plastic half-gallons we'd used previously. What's happening now? I wondered.

In discussing the dilemma with our manufacturer, we remembered that the chai had bonded with peppers in the filling equipment's plastic tubing. Bingo. This off-flavor smelled and tasted just like plastic. Could the chai be assimilating this odd taste from the plastic? I phoned our supplier.

"The half-gallon containers you purchased are not food grade," the rep said, "but manufactured for holding detergents and diesel oil."

How could this happen? I had ordered the same number two plastic, just like our pints and quarts. But what I hadn't realized was that even though the containers were number two plastic, they were just a bit different.

"The plastic taste might be more noticeable in some containers than in others," the representative said.

I guessed that the supplier hadn't known that chai was a food product or, like our honey supplier, felt it wouldn't matter and didn't mention the fact that they were not food grade.

"Well, is there any way I can get food-grade containers and be assured that the chai won't pick up that funny taste?" I asked.

"No," he said bluntly, offering no explanation.

So we dumped more chai.

What were we going to do now? I wondered.

By now, our first manufacturer didn't want much to do with us.

"I never made any money on your product," she told me one day. "And I've decided not to work with you anymore."

I can't say I blame her. She'd invested a lot of money in equipment and lost a lot re-brewing our chai. I was sad to lose her, she had taught me a lot and had worked hard to help us succeed, but I understood her decision. The second processor we were working with agreed they'd keep producing the gallons but, once again, we needed a new location for brewing our smaller quarts and pints - and it might revert back to Carla and me all over again. By this time, we had suspended producing the half-gallons completely, so Carla called the Food Science Department at OSU. The University allowed us the use of their pilot plant, which owned eighty-gallon kettles and filling equipment.

"When can we start?" Carla asked.

We were delighted.

Oregon State University is located in Corvallis, Oregon, about ninety miles south of Portland. While we manufactured there, Carla and I would load both our cars with supplies and be on the road by 6:30 each morning.

The pilot plant was an immense room in an old, brick building. The plant's south facing wall was constructed almost entirely of glass, resembling a huge greenhouse. It was roughly three to four stories high and at least half a block long. Upon our arrival, at about eight a.m., the plant supervisor was always there waiting, kettles fired and ready, smiling and cheerful, providing us both with inspiration.

We loaded our supplies on a large cart and pushed it up a small incline into the building. I thanked God there were no more stairs.

We began brewing by filling the kettles with water. We weighed five-gallon buckets of water with Carla on one side and me on the other. We shoved them toward the pots on a pushcart. Together, we hoisted the water up and over the edge of the kettles. When the pots were filled and the water heating, we measured the ingredients and added them as the water reached a full boil.

After brewing the chai, we each tasted it for accuracy - this was the best part. Carla and I loved sampling the fresh, warm chai. During one particular taste-test, I was reminded of a time from my past when a farmer let me taste fresh milk straight from the cow's udder. I remember it was the best-tasting milk I'd ever had. For me, our chai was just as delicious and about as close to heaven as I could get. Truly, Nirvana in a cup.

One day, we found a dead bee floating in one of the enormous kettles at OSU. The aromas emanating from the pilot plant's kettles were a natural attractant. Still, it was unacceptable and we had to act. The last thing we needed, I thought, is a customer finding an insect swimming in their chai. So, we shielded the kettles with screens.

After brewing the chai, we transferred it into the plant's filling machine. It wasn't as simple as it had been with our first manufacturer where the entire process was automated. Rather than machinery, Carla and I used a five-gallon bucket that we then filled with hot chai. We placed the full bucket onto a cart, wheeled the cart over to the filler, climbed a small ladder, lifted the bucket of hot boiling tea overhead and dumped the chai into the filler's immense funnel. It was a sight to see.

The filler worked by gravity. To fill a bottle, we held it under the spout, stomped on a pedal until the bottle was filled, then capped it by hand. One person filled the bottles and capped them while the other wiped them clean and placed them onto a cart. Then, for cooling, we'd push the cart into an oversized walk-in freezer. When we'd finished filling every bottle, Carla and I would take a well-earned break.

On many afternoons, we walked about eight blocks for the best pizza in the world. Or maybe it was simply because we were both so spent and famished. We'd order a large pizza, sometimes with beer - and we'd eat the whole thing. After lunch, refreshed and full, we'd stroll back to the pilot plant.

Now that the bottles had chilled, we'd wheel the carts back out of the freezer, dry them off, slap on labels and place the containers gently into corrugated boxes. Taped and labeled, we stacked the boxes on a cart, ready for packing into our cars. And every afternoon, before leaving, we'd tidy our mess and ready the plant for the next customer.

I loved cleaning the pilot plant. When the sun shone brightly through its massive windows, it was like toiling in a steam room. A mammoth, black hose that sprayed cool water made the whole process quick and efficient and the tepid water felt good after a hard day's work in that hot, steamy, glass-walled plant.

We sprayed everything, even the tables. The hose's pressure was so powerful that all the bits of leftover ingredients, including the sticky honey, washed swiftly down a drain embedded in the plant's cement floor. It sounds strange, but that hose was my salvation. Just grasping it gave me a sense of closure, relief. We were done, at least for the day.

Oregon Chai's standards insisted upon consistent taste with each batch, so I was always nervous every time we brewed. We couldn't afford any more mistakes. So when I'd turn on that hose, I knew that the process was complete, that I'd done the best job I could. It was as if the jet's stream cleansed away all the day's stored-up anxiety, making my return drive home peaceful, my mind relaxed and renewed.

A friend of mine owned a pet pig. Harvey was his name and he enjoyed our leftover ingredients, gorging himself on anything we'd bring him. He loved it all, leaving nothing behind. One day, my friend noticed Harvey behaving peculiarly and called me on the phone.

"After Harvey gobbled up every last bit," he said, "he acted like he was drunk!"

As if I hadn't already been confused by so many other oddities along our onerous journey, I was yet again perplexed. I wondered what was causing Harvey's eccentricity. Perhaps it was the remnants of caffeine left over from the tea?

But after several repeated episodes with Harvey's odd conduct (a drunken pig is not a pretty sight after all), we decided it best that Harvey not guzzle any more chai scraps. Still, we had to dispose of them somehow.

So we began spreading them in our gardens.

Then, I received a phone call from Carla.

"I've got more flowers in my yard this year!" She insisted.

"And I swear I have fewer slugs!" I said.

Several of our neighborhood friends, as they jogged past our home, also commented on the luscious aroma of the spices wafting up, making their morning regimen all the more enjoyable.

During this time, we met other entrepreneurs at the plant. One company canned brandied peaches and pears, while another dried home-grown cherries then swathed them in chocolate. The owner's package read "Dried Cherries and Chocolate." I later discovered these products on the shelves of the stores where I shopped and was delighted.

After packing our cars with chai, we'd leave early enough so that we could deliver it to our cold storage facility in Portland. There was no more storing it at room temperature. We'd certainly learned that costly lesson.

Carla and I hold many pleasant memories of our time in Corvallis. It was grueling work, but it was fun, too. Sometimes Heather, Lori and Brian would drive up and help us.

Though we enjoyed Brian's company and certainly appreciated his efforts, we disliked his unorthodox method. He preferred using the bottle filler, but after he filled the bottles, he would simply drop the filled containers into a bucket of water, claiming it was easier than wiping them off with a clean towel. The problem with his technique was that we couldn't get the bottles completely dry and when we placed them into the freezer, the excess water on the outside of the containers would freeze solid. Later, when we retrieved the bottles from the freezer, we couldn't remove the moisture and consequently applying the labels was nearly impossible.

After a couple of sessions, we gently relieved Brian of his bottling duties. He didn't mind.

Heather and Lori were helpful, but their minds were on sales and marketing so after a few occasions, they quit coming, too.

Carla and I were not the only ones who benefited from our visits to the pilot plant. Students and staff in Wiegand Hall liked it, too. People would often wander in from other areas of the building just to breathe in the intoxicating brew. It smelled divine.

In May of 1995, Fresh Cup, a trade journal for the coffee and tea industry published an article entitled "High Chai: The Latest Trend in Specialty Tea is More Like a Latte." I was thrilled that the article's first seven paragraphs discussed Oregon Chai.

When I first saw Fresh Cup, I was buying supplies for one of our initial samplings. The magazine was free, so I grabbed one and leafed through it. As I read on, I noticed an ad that eventually led me to our first tea supplier, Devan Shah. Up until this point, I'd been purchasing tea by the pound and Devan offered me the ability to purchase by the 36 kilo or 80 pound burlap bags. It wouldn't be long before we ordered our first full container, shipped straight from its source in India.

The Wall Street Journal called.

At the end of May, a little over a year after Heather and I founded the company, Susan Hauser, a reporter writing a story on Oregon Chai, arrived at our modest office.

Susan poured over Oregon Chai's point of sale materials, fact sheets, distributor lists, press releases and past articles scattered all over our conference room table, Carla's seasoned maple dining room table with her children's initials still carved deeply into its surface.

We worked around her as she interviewed each of our partners. She jotted notes on a white, legal-sized tablet as we filled orders from our desks, planned production and answered her questions between phone calls as we still had no receptionist. Susan was pleasant and calm.

"So," she said, when she got to me. "Tell me what you do."

"Well," I began. "I either spend most of my time at the plant brewing chai or checking inventory levels."

"How did you and Heather start your business?" she asked. "What's it like working with your daughter?"

I smiled and folded my hands in front of me. She was easy to talk to. She had a genuine interest in our company. It was like catching up with an old friend.

"A mother should be so lucky," I said, grinning. "Every day I get to see how she handles the day to day business. I'm proud when she helps customers, making them feel good about taking Oregon Chai and spreading the news about our delicious new product. I get to watch her grow and become an accomplished businesswoman."

As the conversation moved to gardening, I mentioned how I'd spread the steeped spices and tea atop my plants after we'd brewed.

She chuckled and jotted something on her tablet.

The agency Heather and Brian chose wound up doing an outstanding job. Their copywriter had immense talent and we all revered his style.

We'd soon evolved from our initial Himalayan story into his originated: "Oregon Chai is an unapologetically complex mixture of tea and Eros, honey and politics, ginger and contradiction - and the milk of the holy cow. It could be a latte. It could be a tea. But it's not what you think." Customers adored it, often phoning to tell us how much they enjoyed reading our table tents. Many viewed Oregon Chai as "cutting edge," a company willing to be different, willing to take chances.

Acquiring first-class copy and effective design was expensive. Heather was a visionary and displayed a terrific artist's eye, so the graphic designers loved working with her. She and Lori understood high-quality design and knew just what they wanted, but didn't worry about its costs. So, ever the financial conservative, I spoke with our new design agency's CEO and asked that she advise her designers to be more cost conscious.

"We have to stay on budget," I insisted. "Please let your designers know."

Susan's Wall Street Journal article titled "Tea Invades Coffee Country," appeared on Wednesday, June 21, 1995. Everyone at Oregon Chai was excited. My husband sprinted to the local copy shop and made scores of copies of the story. The article was larger than the standard 8.5" X 11" paper, so he printed oversized copies, then cut and pasted a few onto regular, letter-sized paper. He also printed several on buff paper, giving the article an antiqued-tea look. We were so pleased that we displayed copies of the article all over our office. The article was excellent in its description of chai and we relished the addition of the reporter's personal notes. She beautifully narrated Heather's trek through the Himalayas and even how we all insisted that the composted chai we'd sprinkled onto our gardens both increased the number of blooms on Carla's rhododendrons and banished the banana slugs from my yard. We were beside ourselves.

That same month I donned my cap and gown and proudly joined my fellow graduates at commencement where I received my Bachelor's Degree in Liberal Arts. A few weeks later I turned 50!

To increase our product line and make it competitive with other similar drinks, Heather wanted a ready-to-drink beverage. She loved Starbucks' Frappuccino in their adorable mini-bottles but processing and packing in glass was very expensive. We questioned our package supplier, who suggested we test an eight-ounce juice box. We gave that a try.

Blending our chai concentrate with fresh milk, we sent it through the processing system but it tasted scorched. I was disappointed. The plant technicians explained that products often tasted odd initially, but usually improved and might taste better in another week. So we waited.

The small, white eight-ounce aseptic juice boxes were transported from the processing plant to CCI Enterprises, a non-profit organization that provided numerous services, including employment for developmentally disabled adults. CCI employees applied new, blue Oregon Chai labels to our charming, little containers. When they finished, the pallets of the new ready-to-drink beverage were delivered to our office.

We were all anxious as re-sampling time arrived. We wanted this product to succeed. We just knew our customers would love it. The tiny boxes looked great. We gathered around to taste the chai. Everybody grabbed a container, stripped the plastic straw off the back, pierced the top and slowly started sipping. But the scalded taste remained, overwhelming the chai flavors. We were all disappointed.

Devan, our tea vendor, turned out to be a real prize. He generously offered us two feet inside his booth at the New York Fancy Food Show for the following July. This was a major breakthrough for us. We couldn't afford a booth or a membership in N.A.S.F.T., but we were committed to making the absolute most out of those precious two feet he'd allotted us.

Our challenge was conceiving a display appropriate for such a tiny space. My husband, fortunately for us an architect by trade, conceived the construction of an exhibit table using a one-foot-square television tray.

I created a three-sided fitted canvas skirt to cover the tray he designed. He then laminated our point of sale materials and hung them from metal rings so that they dangled from the table's frame, leaving its one-foot square tabletop free for chai samples.

Heather and Brian would have to take turns standing within the remaining one foot of space. It was a brilliant conception.

In July, Heather and Brian flew to New York. Still limited by a lack of funds, they lodged with Brian's parents in their Manhattan apartment. For increased exposure, Lori prepared press kits for them to leave strategically in the international gourmet food show's pressroom.

Even though we only squeaked out a miniscule presence, our exposure was wildly successful and priceless. Newsweek picked up our press kit and on 8/14/95, just a couple months after our great coverage in The Wall Street Journal, they published an article entitled "Hot Cha Cha, Hot Cha Chai," featuring a photo of our eight-ounce, ready-to-drink container. None of us had any idea where they'd gotten that picture, since this particular product wasn't even available, as we hadn't even worked out all the kinks yet. But, as they say, any press is good press. A great feature article - even with a photo of a not-yet-available product - was invaluable, helping spread the word nationally.

C H A P T E R   1 3

Trade Shows: One Lump? Or Two?

Everyone was now convinced that trade shows should become our marketing priority. In August, just one and one-half years after Heather and I had founded Oregon Chai, we rented our first booth at the North American Specialty Coffee and Beverage Retailers' Expo, commonly referred to as "NASCORE" to be held at the Oregon Convention Center.

Heather wanted our presentation meticulous, desiring a professional look for our display. But, as before, we still had little money for an elaborate exhibit. Whatever we needed, we'd have to create ourselves.

With her innate sense of style, Heather said she disliked the royal-blue curtains that were draped throughout the convention center's immense room.

"I want a more natural look for our booth," she insisted.

"Yes," I agreed. "I can sew muslin curtains and matching tablecloths."

The day before the trade show opened, I brewed a sizeable batch of our tea. Then David and I joined Heather in the exhibit hall to assemble our booth. David and I hung the new curtains I'd made while Heather dressed the tables.

Heather had ordered an oversized bouquet of flowers as a centerpiece. We dressed the table around it with business cards and table tents. We hung laminated media articles in striking, four-color print on the booth's backdrop. I stepped back and peered at our booth. It was warm and welcoming, just the way Heather wanted.

We returned home to greet Devan and his wife who were staying with us during the show. They'd also rented a booth and would be making a presentation on tea, including a sampling of over thirty exotic teas from all around the world. We sipped glasses of wine and visited for a while. Then I excused myself to bottle the chai for the next day.

I had to reheat the chai to near boiling in order to pasteurize it. I grabbed a large, glass pitcher and filled it with the steaming hot brew. Typically, I warmed the pitcher before pouring in the hot liquid. But this time, apparently overly fatigued, I wasn't thinking clearly. As I filled the carafe with hot chai, it suddenly exploded, sending glass shards dangerously about the kitchen followed by splatters of the scalding liquid. As Murphy would have it, it was a summer night and I was in shorts and flip flops. The boiling chai blistered my legs as pieces of glass sliced into my calves and feet, cutting deep into one of my toes.

"David!" I yelled. "Help!"

My husband and guests raced in. They saw my bloodied foot and quickly wrapped it in a towel and carried me to the car. With my foot resting on the dashboard of my husband's cramped Miata, we sped to the hospital emergency room.

A doctor plucked bits and pieces of glass from both of my legs and stitched up my toe. I felt horrible. I'm going to miss our first trade show, I thought. But I felt even worse for being so absentminded to have foolishly poured the scorching chai into a room temperature glass pitcher in the first place. I knew better than that. When I returned home, my gracious guests had completely cleaned up our kitchen: glass, chai and blood - all gone.

The next day I hobbled to our booth on crutches, plopped myself in a corner and watched Heather and Brian greet our visitors and hand out samples of Oregon Chai. They were both smiling and enthusiastic. We had no heating equipment, so we served chilled samples in plastic cups by pouring milk and chai over ice.

It was summer, so having the iced drink actually worked out nicely. Hoards of curious patrons crowded our booth, welcoming the cool refreshment. I was thrilled but I couldn't stay long. So I went home, plunked my aching foot atop a pillow and waited anxiously to hear from Heather to see how we did by day's end.

"The trade show was a huge success!" she said when she finally called that evening. "We got lots of new customers and everyone was talking about Oregon Chai!"

My foot throbbed but I was delighted.

We started receiving calls from customers in several other states. The first came from a woman working as a flight attendant. When she wasn't flying, she worked in an espresso bar at a ski resort in Colorado. On one of her many trips to Portland she tried Oregon Chai and loved it instantly. When she returned home, she discussed Oregon Chai with the owner of the espresso bar where she worked. They decided they'd offer it to their customers and ordered a case. We were excited about getting an order from another state - but now we had to figure out how we'd ship them their chai.

Heather and I both loved skiing, but neither of us could justify the expense of hand-delivering the chai ourselves just to get up on the mountain - much as we'd have loved to. Our territory was finally expanding beyond our distributors' territory or our ability to deliver from out of the backs of our trunks. Which opened up the challenges of how to ship this heavy, liquid product?

Oregon Chai was perpetually financially strapped, so we always had to come up with creative solutions - and shipping strategies would be no different.

Rather than buy brand new shipping boxes, I swallowed my pride and strolled though our neighborhood asking other businesses if they had any good cardboard boxes they didn't need. Some, of course, were way too large, but I was able to trim these down and tape them together into the right size and shape. And while I was embarrassed by the Frankenstein appearance of our make-shift strategy, I was willing to make a go of it if they worked. Which they didn't. The whole exercise was a total waste of time as they fell apart, their integrity challenged; they were incapable of supporting the weight of forty-five pounds of chai. We had no choice but to break down and buy corrugated shipping boxes.

Still ever-searching for the best deal, I located a supplier that sold used boxes at a reasonable discount. They worked fine except for the erroneous printing covering each one made shipping errors a constant worry. We used these for a short time until we eventually found a supplier who would sell us small quantities of corrugated boxes at large-quantity discounts.

For our new, out-of-state customers, we experienced another major hurdle: our product required refrigeration, which meant we had to pack everything in dry ice. This was turning into a major hassle but if we were going to grow, we had to cut our teeth somewhere.

We had no way of storing dry ice, consequently we had to make almost daily visits to our ice supplier to facilitate our ever-increasing out-of-state shipping demands. The dry ice was difficult to handle. We had to wear heavy gloves so the ice wouldn't burn our hands. If I forgot my gloves, I'd try wrapping several pieces of newspaper around each block, but this method was inefficient as the slippery blocks would simply slide right out of the paper. We needed a better system.

Since our chai was a heavy product, the addition of shipping prices to our product was also a concern. I researched pricing and soon learned that if we had one basic price, people living on the West Coast would pay too much for the chai, while those residing on the East Coast wouldn't pay enough. And the discrepancy in pricing wouldn't cover our costs anyway - so everyone lost. We tried establishing a price based upon time zones. It worked for a while. Ultimately, we computerized our shipping system and charged one standard price for our chai and simply added the actual shipping charges to the base rate.

Trade Shows: Metallic Bladders and Sweet Dreams

Aseptic containers presented themselves as the only remaining viable option to our packaging problems. And since we needed to fill a five-thousand-gallon minimum production requirement, that meant increased expenses - we suddenly needed about a quarter of a million dollars to take a step in any direction.

We were just hemorrhaging cash it seemed. When would it end? How could we ever come up with the cash we needed to in order to stay in business? It was obvious we had no choice but to make the shift over to aseptic packaging as quickly as possible. But how would we ever afford it?

Fortunately, Brian's business plan solicitations, that he'd been working on diligently and persistently since he came on board, finally panned out. He successfully secured us $150,000 from a private investor. Though we had wanted - and needed - a quarter of a million, we happily took what we could get.

Safe packaging was obviously our #1 priority. Brian began an extensive search, finally discovering a 1.5-gallon bag-in-a-box, resembling those used for wine and a one liter aseptic box, like the containers used for non-refrigerated soy milk.

He thought these containers would work great but they required sophisticated equipment that was only available at large processing and packing companies. So Brian kept searching.

He hunted for several weeks, finally locating a suitable match, but still not finding a company that could brew our tea as well as package it. Consequently, our processor would have to brew the tea then ship it via a tanker truck to an entirely different plant for packaging. It was a roundabout process but it was certainly worth the hassle.

When we moved to aseptic cartons, our package design received a complete overhaul. My son, Sean, conceived of a pattern of glasses filled with chai on a brightly colored background. Ever detail-oriented, Lori diligently examined colors searching for just the perfect hues that would capture the essence of this centuries-old beverage in contemporary colors.

The agency employed this suggestion, creating an Indian-inspired repeating pattern of tiny cups coupled with a sun motif atop a yellow background on the box's upper diagonal and tiny cups coupled with a snowflake motif atop a purple background on its lower half. It was the perfect visual cue that chai is delicious served hot or cold.

We had also discovered that some of our customers didn't understand the instructions printed on the packaging. To simplify and clarify how to prepare chai from our concentrate, my husband drew a small picture of an Oregon Chai container and a carton of milk both pouring equal parts simultaneously into a pitcher demonstrating the universally understood 50/50 combination. Lori refined his concept and replicated his illustration on a computer.

Heather also wanted information printed on the box telling consumers that the container was recyclable. Initially, recycling of the aseptic containers was only available in a few states. To help customers find out where to take their empty containers for recycling, we included the toll-free phone number, then the website address for information. Our ingenious copy-writer included the statement, "Remember - it's a small planet, but you wouldn't want to paint it."

The first time we manufactured at the new plant, Carla and I arrived at six a.m. and immediately checked the raw ingredients. As we had requested, they'd arrived the previous day. I never wanted to have an entire crew standing around waiting for my ingredients (or me) ever again. It looked and smelled delicious. We were ready to go.

The crew prepared the kettles and began to heat the water. Carla and I perched on catwalks and watched the mahogany liquid swirl in mammoth whirlpools around the giant kettles, blending itself into our favorite beverage. It reminded me of dark, bittersweet chocolate and I felt like Charlie in Willie Wonka and the Chocolate Factory. The building teemed with the aroma of exotic spices, with the scent of sweet honey and the perfume of Indian black teas. I was excited and pleased with how everything was working out.

The brewing was time-consuming but we knew we had to be patient with the steeping process - it could not be rushed. Besides, it beat preparing eight gallons at a time on a church kitchen stovetop - at that rate, we would've had to brew for 625 non-stop hours - or about twenty-six continuous days to match this batch. I was glad to be outsourcing, to be sure.

In between batches, Carla and I waited in the company's conference room, seated at a large, maple meeting table. The room offered just one small row of windows placed way too high to catch a view and nothing but a handful of sorely outdated magazines. The staff offered us a television but without cable, we were left with only accounting and software video tutorials that didn't pique our interest. But it didn't matter. We were too nervous to concentrate on anything but the brewing anyhow, so we passed most of the time chatting and joking.

As day faded to night, Carla and I became increasingly fatigued. With no couches or comfy chairs in that immense, cave-like room, propriety eventually gave out to weariness and we both simply lay down on the soft azure blue carpet.

I doubt if even five minutes passed before we were both fast asleep.

When the crew finished our chai and returned to the conference room to alert us, they found two middle-aged women in white lab coats and paper hairnets, sprawled, passed out, exhausted. I awoke to drool dripping silently onto the carpet beneath me. Carla stirred across the room and grinned at me. It might've been the first real sleep either of us had had in a long time, knowing our baby is being safely taken care of nearby.

Our chai was finally pumped into a tanker and readied for shipping. I headed home and after a few more hours of real sleep in my own bed, I climbed back into my car and headed for the plant where our sweet concentrate would be packaged.

The drive took me several hours. When I finally arrived, I missed the freeway exit completely, driving right past the town. I exited a mile or so later and slowly maneuvered my way back through town to the plant.

I was concerned I was late. When I drove into the parking lot, I saw an enormous empty loading dock at the end of the building that could accommodate four or five semi-trucks. Next to the loading dock was a small office. Thinking I shouldn't park in front of the loading dock in case a semi arrived, I drove past the building, through a gate and into a graveled lot where several cars were parked.

After combing my hair and daubing on a bit of lipstick, I entered the office where a receptionist waited. I introduced myself. She was pleasant and pointed me toward the filling area where our chai was being processed. I strolled into the first large warehouse and saw finished products stacked neatly on pallets in several long rows.

Inside the second warehouse, an automated line filled canned soft drinks. I was surprised how quiet the plant was and how few people it employed. A couple of employees sat in the lunchroom, but I saw no one else. At the far end of the third warehouse, I finally found what I was looking for: atop a high platform lay the packing equipment filling and boxing our Oregon Chai concentrate. Five workers were all that was necessary. At last, I thought, no more screwing on caps by hand!

"Hello!" I called out. But no one answered. A few heads nodded but no one really acknowledged my presence.

I continued wandering about when finally a couple of workers spoke with me: the Shipping Manager, the Vice President of Sales and the Quality Control Manager, who took hourly samples of our chai to the lab for testing.

I was allowed to roam around as much as I liked, not needing a visitor pass or even a hairnet. No one seemed concerned about what I saw or where I went. I assumed they either completely trusted me or knew that I had no idea what I was seeing, let alone being capable of detailing it to anyone else. Their attitude surprised me completely. At our manufacturing plant, the director cautioned that everything we saw or heard was confidential and that we should never divulge any information. It was a refreshing change.

I watched the containers as they were filled. The method was worlds apart from the manual process we'd been using up until this time. Afterward, the hefty, metallic bladders were dropped onto a short, sloping conveyor belt where they traversed two or three feet to another belt. There, a worker heaved each filled bag into its box.

The boxes then traveled around a bend, were flipped over, sealed, dated and disappeared through a hole in the wall where another worker stacked them onto a pallet. A forklift transferred the filled pallet into another room where all the pallets filled with chai boxes sat lined up in neatly spaced rows. It was magical.

I gazed at the rows of uniform pallets filled with Oregon Chai. I felt secure. Our chai was brewed, had survived the lengthy trip in its tanker, was packaged carefully into safe aseptic containers and now waited ready for shipment to our customers. I breathed in, exhaled and then headed out for a lunch reprieve.

After eating, I strolled around downtown. After an hour or so, I headed back to the plant and observed the same automated magical routine. In just one short year, I thought to myself, we've evolved from manually packing 16-gallons worth of plastic bottles at a church to this sophisticated, smooth operation. I was satisfied. And I was tired. Drained from both the night before and the long drive that morning, I decided I had best just find a motel close by and crash, I was simply too tired to make the trek home after such an exhausting couple of days. I drove to one I'd spotted earlier that day and checked in. Sleep came easily knowing we had competent packagers and safe, new containers. All of our problems, it seemed, had been resolved.

CHAPTER 15

The Dalai Lama

After our first day with the new manufacturer, Carla and I were moved from the conference room into a smaller room within the main plant adjacent to the kettles. This room was used as a mini laboratory for quick product testing such as pH or color.

As I sat watching the brewing, I noticed that the line was backed up and chai was seeping onto the floor. No one else noticed. I went for help and the situation was quickly resolved. Still, the next time we visited the plant, we were asked to wait in the main laboratory's office building.

"I don't think they liked my getting involved," I told Carla.

But Carla and I were fine with that. We weren't sit around and do nothing kind of women. We actually preferred to be stationed in the main lab because more people were around. We watched them working and chatted with many of them. It was much more enjoyable than being cooped up by ourselves, bird's eye view or no.

On September 13, 1995, the Seattle Post published a feature article on Oregon Chai. In the piece, the owner of Plenty, an upscale food shop and storefront café in Seattle, Washington, described our original concentrate as: "incredibly comforting...The buzz you get is better than with coffee...It's a clean high."

Soon after we started marketing Oregon Chai concentrate in the 1.5 gallon units, we were finally able to start packing our retail containers in aseptic liters - no more plastic! When the big day arrived I went to the office at our new co-packers where the manager greeted me and escorted me to their lab. There I was introduced to the food scientists who would supervise the packing. I put on a white lab coat and hairnet and followed them into the plant where huge sophisticated equipment waited ready to start processing.

I watched the crew wash the line where our sweet chai would flow to the filling equipment. After cleansing, they rinsed the system completely with sterilized water then flushed the water from the system using the Oregon Chai concentrate.

A lab technician took samples of the heavily-diluted-with-water chai mixture while holding the edge of the two-inch diameter pipe over a drain in the floor. I watched as the liquid changed from clear water to a light, caramel brown to a darker, chestnut hue. The technician checked the concentration level by using an instrument called a brix meter and as the mixture approached its target, it finally emerged the beautiful, luscious dark brown of our delectable chai.

As I viewed our beverage being expelled down the drain all I could think about was how much chai we were wasting. I was upset if I spilled a cup - this was more like a few hundred gallons! I felt lightheaded, I worried I'd collapse. I breathed deeply and tried to get hold of myself. Fortunately, the sensation quickly passed. The containers started filling as thousands of elfin Oregon Chai cartons advanced down the line.

I beamed with pride, these were my babies. The scene reminded me of a three-year-old performing at her first dance recital with all the other toddlers, tapping their little feet, marching in a row on stage. A lump formed in my throat as I muffled an emotional sob.

As I stood there in awe, trying to control myself, the food technicians showed me the charts tracking various measurements. Though I had no idea what I was seeing and knew nothing of what they tracked, I was thrilled, thankful for their help, grateful for their expertise and happy beyond belief. Once again, I thought, we're safe. I don't need to worry any more. From now on everything will be fine, won't it?

For the aseptic retail package, Heather, Brian and Lori came up with the idea of adding a brief note about the Dalai Lama on each carton.

It read: "Manufactured for Oregon Chai Inc., Portland, Oregon, 97209, without the consent of the Dalai Lama, but we sent him a case and some Three Stooges movies so we expect to hear from him soon."

I was concerned.

"I'm afraid that our customers might think we're trying to profit by using the Dalai Lama's name."

"Don't worry Mom," she replied. "I think it will make more people aware of the Tibetans' plight and customers will get a kick out of the reference."

Heather was right. We received only one or two phone calls from customers saying they thought the reference was inappropriate. The rest enjoyed it.

Ever-resourceful and daring, Heather even wrote to the Dalai Lama, himself - and included with the letter some of our newly aseptically packaged Oregon Chai concentrate and Three Stooges videos to make it legit.

Her note read:

```
January 17, 1996
Dalai Lama
Office of His Holiness
Thekchen Choeling
McLeod Ganj
Dharamsala H.P., India 176219


Dear Dalai Lama:
My name is Heather McMillen and I would like you to
accept this small gift.  I would be honored if you would
try my chai.  The Three Stooges movies are also yours to
enjoy (we heard you liked them).
     I visited India in 1989 and became a hopeless chai
addict.  I loved it so much I decided to try making my own
version here in Oregon.  My friends loved that so much
that my mother and I decided to try making a business of
it.  Oregon Chai is the product of our efforts.  I hope
you like it.  It is a bit different than the chai I drank
in India.  I use only honey to sweeten it, lots of vanilla
bean and cinnamon along with a bunch of other ingredients
such as fresh ginger.
     You might notice that we have mentioned you on our
package.  I hope this is all right.  You are a global symbol
of not only Asia, but of strength, history and peace.  I
wouldn't claim that our chai is all of those things, but
I think that if Americans can find humor in something so
seemingly foreign (like a product with a foreign name or
a displaced culture in the face of political aggression),
```

they might develop a sense of awareness and global community almost subconsciously. We have to make things easy for people over here.

To prepare the chai add milk (equal parts milk and chai) and heat it or ice it. Please let us know if you or any of your friends would like more. You may call us collect. Thank you and enjoy the chai!

Sincerely,

Heather McMillen and everyone else at Oregon Chai, Inc.

Shortly after, we received a letter from one of the local monks expressing that the Dalai Lama had received and enjoyed our Oregon Chai.

Speed to Market - We Found Our Guy

Sales calls, especially for a new, unknown product are demanding. But Heather had a natural affinity for it. Her outgoing, honest personality drew people in. They liked her and they were willing to listen. Still, successful sales require more than simple friendliness.

Heather's responsibilities were growing daily. During our opening year, Heather was practically alone in her quest for customers. We had to push to get the Oregon Chai brand to market before our competition learned too much about our product, copied it and got theirs to market, too. We needed someone who knew which companies would be the optimum matches for our product and which stores catered to the Oregon Chai customer. It was a race.

Building our sales team in order to support her in meeting our monthly, quarterly and annual goals emerged as her chief priority. Heather's goal was one million in sales per month. And she wanted even more.

In order to accomplish her target, we needed to build our market presence and strengthen our organization. Though we had done gangbusters on our own in terms of sales and marketing, we knew we could do better with some experienced guidance. Access to crucial distributors required professional help from an expert offering both more experience and richer contacts. So Heather set out in search of a sales consultant and regional manager to help take us to the next level.

In September of 1995, we found our guy: Dwight Sinclair. Bright and enthusiastic with over eleven years of food industry experience, Dwight had been the Vice President of Marketing for another Oregon company and had grown their sales exponentially. A dedicated sales person, he was familiar with distribution and already had well-developed business relationships with many of the key players in the natural products industry: our main retail market. We invited him to our office as an industry consultant.

He arrived, dressed impeccably in a fine suit and tie. With shirtsleeves rolled to his elbows, he offered fresh ideas and unwavering enthusiasm. He stood in front of our blackboard, his mind on overdrive, scratching out formulas, explaining how pricing worked and describing distributor and retail outlet markup to our ravenous ears.

"I'm concerned about your pricing structure," he said finally. "We have to modify it. I want to institute volume pricing."

We changed that immediately.

"Next, you need to get a data base software program," he said, still scribbling out ideas on the chalkboard.

Up until that very moment, I'd kept track of our customers in Word, which I knew was inefficient, but our budget didn't allow for software upgrades. Turns out, I didn't have much of a choice in the matter. Call it fate kicking me in the butt to get up to speed. I was away manufacturing when my shared computer crashed. It was toted away to be rebuilt - losing a thousand contacts and six months of laborious work in the process. No time like the present to start a new system, I rationalized, trying to make lemonade out of the lemons that had suddenly been squished in my face.

Before Dwight joined us, we'd secured only six distributors. We needed more!

October 1995, was also a milestone in our growth. We got our first paychecks! A long, long time coming. And Lori finally came on board full-time. She took over all the packaging details and I gladly never gave any of that another thought.

A few months before Dwight joined us we contracted with another consultant to provide us with some badly needed accounting expertise. We initiated an advisory board consisting of our original five founding members and these two consultants. While our five founders continued to meet weekly, the seven of us met at least once a month and it was within these advisory board meetings that our strategic decisions were developed.

Our vendors and distributors continued asking our sales team about the availability of new products. Specifically, they wanted products with increased accessibility, like a ready-to-drink chai. Not being a food scientist, but being the R & D department by default, I took it upon myself to figure out ways to expand our product line.

I was elated when I found an out-of-state research facility where we could test small batches of ready-to-drink chai variations. The facility was expensive, ten thousand dollars for one day's use. I spent several weeks chatting on the phone with a food scientist debating the investment and discussing the details of our experiment. I knew you get what you pay for and considering our trial and error track record thus far, I hoped their expertise and state of the art equipment might shorten and lessen our learning curve.

When I arrived at the test lab, I learned from an employee that the food scientist I'd been speaking with for several weeks was out for the day, and only technicians were available to help. Gulp!

Okay, I rationalized, placating my own fears, maybe this is just standard operating procedure and I don't need to have my hand held. I'm sure they're all equally qualified and the food scientist would've just been overseeing their process and I'd be working with the technicians all day anyway. I suppressed my fears and proceeded.

What I hadn't understood was that facility employees were only there to operate the equipment. I was supposed to have any formula issues resolved before testing. I felt abandoned and confused. I had spent all this money securing the lab and paying for airfare to get their help to test and develop this new product. Wasn't that what I'd come for? Now I was on my own with no one to help me?

As I pondered my situation, the receptionist presented a big platter full of fresh fruit and muffins.

"Help yourself," she said.

What a nice gesture, I thought.

"Oh, thank you," I said, helping myself to her generous offering.

A little food in my stomach improved my outlook. Since I couldn't un-reserve the plant the day of, the money invested was non-refundable, and the equipment was sitting at the ready, I figured I had better make the best of my situation.

The technicians and I went ahead with a couple of tests. They packaged the chai in small, eight-ounce containers. After several hours of work, the staff invited me for a delicious, hour-long lunch of tossed salad, spaghetti and garlic bread.

These people are so fortunate, I thought. They work in such a nice place and have all these great meals available. The receptionist even took a quick nap after lunch. She told me later that day that she woke at five a.m. and didn't get home from work at night until well after seven and that bit of rest allowed her more waking time with her family in the evenings. I was impressed.

After lunch we completed our tests. Satisfied, I left the facility and flew home to Portland. The ready-to-drink chai we had (hopefully) perfected would be shipped after the technicians finished testing that the seals to the containers would resist mold, yeast and bacterial growth.

When the test packets arrived at our office, everyone gathered around and snatched a container and together we each opened one. We sipped, eagerly hoping for success.

"They taste burned!" Heather said, disappointed.

I sipped mine. She was right. The milk had scalded. The test was a bust. Our ready-to-drink was not ready to drink. But that wasn't the only issue. Included with the hefty invoice for the testing was a bill for the food - not only for me - but for each and every employee at the facility the entire day I had been there!

"No wonder they were so nice," I said, rolling my eyes. "I treated everyone to their fruit tray breakfasts and spaghetti lunch."

I was astonished. Not only did I not get what I thought I had paid an exorbitant amount of money for, but they had stuck me with the bill for everyone's meals. I immediately called the company and protested fervently.

"I didn't order any food," I said.

"It's customary," the receptionist said. "Our regular customers are used to this arrangement."

"Well, I'm not one of your regular customers," I blurted out. "And I'm certainly not used to it! I had no idea. No one ever bothered to mention it to me!"

After debating for over an hour, the food charge was begrudgingly removed from our invoice. I was astounded at how unfulfilled my expectations had been. Still, we had nothing - except yet another costly lesson learned.

Brian pursued the ready-to-drink product as a joint venture with another company already up and running in that arena - and they were willing to finance more reformulation and tests.

They loaned us their food scientist, a woman who understood chemistry and knew what levels of milk fat and emulsifier would provide the best flavor and texture. I met with her at the University of Utah. The facility's equipment was smaller but their fees were proportionately lower.

The food scientist and I initiated a couple of tests and broke at noon for lunch. This time, I bought my own food in the university's cafeteria. No more surprises for me, I thought.

After the break, we ran a few more tests. When I returned home, I waited nervously but hopefully for the results.

Finally, two weeks later, our samples arrived. Half were delivered to our office and the rest to our distributor who had funded the venture, where they conducted a taste test focus group with two hundred participants. Out of the five flavor variations we'd experimented with, the distributor found one that nearly everyone enjoyed - but the flavor still did not meet Heather's high standards.

I returned to Utah, on my own and tried one more time. Despite my efforts, this ready-to-drink chai was also unsatisfactory. When did I become a food science recipe developer? I asked myself. I was frustrated. I really didn't enjoy this part of the business at all. Not remotely. I was ill equipped for this task and had no real interest in pursuing further education. Still, there was no one else to do it. So I thought to myself, we'll work on getting this responsibility fielded out to someone more qualified but in the interim, it's my solitary domain. So, what can I do next?

No matter what we did, we just couldn't get the flavor robust enough to cover the burnt milk taste that troubled Heather so much. I kept plugging away at it. I wondered if I could do just one thing, maybe I'd be able to close the loop - but we had such a small staff, we all had to wear so many hats, I couldn't focus exclusively on recipe development while I was trying to keep the doors open, and manufacture the chai. It was overwhelming - and yet still exhilarating and stimulating. I was proud of all that we had accomplished - and the promise of what lay ahead. Thus, our ready-to-drink development was set unofficially on a back burner. Luckily our talented sales team had plenty to keep them occupied moving several thousand servings of Oregon Chai concentrate into the hands of anxiously waiting consumers.

CHAPTER 17

Getting Tipsy Over Chai Mai Tai

As we grew, all of our marketing material evolved from computer-generated data into polished, professionally designed and printed pieces. Lori was meticulous about maintaining a clippings file. She watched local and national newspapers and key magazines like a hawk, always looking for articles on or referencing Oregon Chai.

She had them professionally reprinted on rich, glossy paper for use in both press and sales kits. They also doubled as elegant handouts for the numerous trade shows and presentations we conducted.

As another marketing tool, I tried to contact our customers as often as possible to show them that we cared and appreciated their business without overwhelming them with unwanted materials.

In particular I liked sending out Christmas cards. During our first couple of years, since our budget was always severely limited, I just placed a couple of recipes on a 4"x 6" card and mailed them as a special, personal touch.

The idea soon caught on. A couple of years later, our marketing department was designing and mailing out stylish holiday cards encompassing the very same concept. Necessity truly is the mother of invention.

Every time I read a recipe in a magazine, I thought, how could I convert this for use with our chai concentrate? I created recipes for some wonderful flavored drinks - and one miserable mushroom soup, which rightly, ended up down the garbage disposal.

Heather often teased me about my voice mail messages, calling me "Betty Crocker" because I'd vary my outgoing message to add things like: "Oregon Chai is great over ice cream." I knew that most people deplored waiting through long recordings just to leave a message, but a handful mentioned how much they liked Oregon Chai splashed atop their ice cream and I wanted to take advantage of every opportunity to make our customers aware of its other various applications.

We hired an award-winning chef, Polly Schoonmaker (now Wood), who produced a variety of applications including spritzers, cream sodas, smoothies, cantaloupe frappé and some delicious and decadent mixed drinks. Each was delicious. My favorite was the Chai Mai Tai. We had a lot of fun trying her creations.

Another chef friend, Maggie, a young woman employed with our manufacturer's research and development department, was responsible for creating possible uses for the various fruits they processed in the plant. She crafted lots of miniature fruit nuggets that were useful in baking and often gave Carla and I samples as part of her internal taste tests to determine which piece offered the best flavor and color.

She was a phenomenal cook and made remarkable desserts from next to nothing. For one employee's birthday, she was asked to prepare something special with very little notice. She rummaged through her cupboards, grabbed a handful of ingredients and, like a magician, produced a marvelous chocolate, coconut and fruit bar.

One day, Carla and I were distressed to find Maggie weeping in her office. She was upset, angered with her supervisor, a woman whom Carla and I both knew as kind.

"I can't continue working like this," she said, wiping her eyes. "It's just too much."

We didn't know what the situation was and didn't make it our business. It's kind of a given that we all have bad days and its no shock that many employees often hate where they work, regardless of what outsiders might perceive. Admittedly, the plant was so busy that everyone worked long hours. As in most firms, there was always too much to do and not enough people to get it done. Still, we wanted to cheer her up.

"I want to start my own business." Maggie told us. "Maybe a bakery or something."

Carla and I both knew that if she didn't try, she'd probably regret it for the rest of her life.

"You should absolutely go for it," we told her. We praised her on her amazing culinary skills and encouraged her to pursue her dreams.

"But I'm afraid," she said. "I've always worked for someone else."

After a few months of continued championing from us, she finally made the dramatic move.

She opened her own café in Forest Grove and named it "Maggie's Buns." Shortly after - and certainly no surprise to us - a local newspaper rated her cinnamon buns a ten on a scale of one to ten as the best cinnamon buns in the region.

In just a few short months she'd hired a sizeable staff, offered great food and boasted a café packed with customers. We even saw her rollerblading around town on sunny afternoons, looking much cheerier than the weepy girl we'd seen just a few months earlier. We were proud that our entrepreneurial success had encouraged another woman to pursue her dreams.

By January of 1996, we'd paid out over thirty-eight thousand dollars in marketing expenses with an outstanding balance on our fifty thousand dollar contract of thirteen thousand. I asked repeatedly that the agency stay on budget and felt that their staff had convinced ours that we needed overly expensive designs.

They produced four-color stationery boasting a banner of print along the page's bottom and each page included double-sided printing. They reasoned that printing on both sides was essential since the message reading across the bottom of the page was "circular" stating: "you come to your senses and fill the void that changes your mind and opens your eyes so you come to your senses and fill the void that changes your mind, etc., etc., etc..."

As clever as this copy was, each piece of paper cost us fifty cents. Through previous research, I had discovered that start-ups require only business cards and a one-color catalog and wondered if all this was really necessary. I felt that instead of guiding us into an economical program, the agency's designers were going crazy at our expense. It's also possible I just hadn't gotten used to the idea yet that we were maturing beyond the start-up phase.

One afternoon, our account rep ordered business cards for everyone and showed me an example. They were flashy but I didn't like that our phone number was on the front and our address was on the back. It didn't make sense to me. Why wasn't all my contact information on the same side? So I phoned the designer.

"From my experience," I said, "I know how annoying it is to have to take a card out of the Rolodex and turn it over. Would you please put all the information on one side? It will save everybody a lot of trouble."

"Well," our rep answered, "our agency's manager doesn't want to print your cards that way."

I was shocked. Who was the customer here? Shouldn't the decision-maker be the one footing the fifty thousand dollar bill?

"Your manager doesn't want to print them that way?" I asked, astounded.

Frustrated, I rolled the card over and over in my hand.

"That's fine," I said. "I'll just have them printed somewhere else."

I couldn't believe it. I was the customer. Just give me what I want, please.

Despite all of our stunning new marketing materials, Lori still had reservations. She came into my office one day.

"Are we limiting ourselves by calling the company 'Oregon' Chai?" she asked.

I was so busy brewing chai, conducting taste-tests, doing daily accounting reports, processing orders, helping cutomers, managing the office and running the Board of Directors that the last thing I needed was to figure out another name for our chai - and reprint all of our packaging and start from scratch again marketing and promoting a new name. It was inconceivable to me to even think about changing our name.

That had been settled before we even started. Who among us had the time to even think about how much time, money and effort would go into re-branding ourselves and making a splash big enough to compete with our own former name recognition? I mean, we were, after all, the industry leader with an overwhelming market share. If it ain't broke, don't fix it, I figured. We had enough problems to deal with - our name, certainly, wasn't one of them.

"It was the name Heather chose," I said abruptly. "And I don't want to change it."

"It sounds foreign," Lori explained. "Will it prevent people from trying it?"

She had wondered about the word chai itself. Not many people even knew what chai was. These were rational, legitimate questions and Lori certainly had a point. But everyone was so occupied with other affairs that changing our name was not a priority.

I honestly didn't even give Lori a chance to fully express her concern.

The name stayed.

Regrettably, the exclusive agreement we had signed with our first distributor resulted in a crisis.

We had grown even faster than anyone could've anticipated and, in a little over a year, one of the largest natural products distributors offered to carry Oregon Chai. This was a tremendous opportunity, one we knew we needed.

Their distribution area covered the entire West Coast and everything west of the Mississippi River. The major dilemma was that they required distributorship in the area already serviced by our first distributor. We tried working out an arrangement satisfying both our local and national distributors, but we just couldn't please everyone.

Our local distributor became upset, afraid he'd lose the business he'd worked so hard to build. This was a fair concern but we couldn't let his size or limitations hold us back. Our own business was our priority, not his. We had simply outgrown him.

We offered him a royalty on every case the larger company distributed within his territory through the end of his contract - but he refused.

We finally had no choice but to come out of pocket with $25,000 to buy back his contract. This put us further into debt but we hoped we would make it up in the enhanced sales from the new, larger, major distributor.

In February of 1996, Brian miraculously found us another four hundred and fifty thousand in venture capital. This second round of financing was such a boost. It's amazing how money - or rather, the lack thereof, can strangle a small business from soaring to great heights. I know that our scraping by and creative resourcefulness had taught us terrific skills in the first lean year or two, but this almost half a million dollars launched us into a whole new league. Now we were really on our way.

Our advisory board decided we needed a new approach to our marketing material.

Again.

Jeeze.

It seemed like every time I turned around, more money got poured into marketing.

Our current items were cutting-edge and clever but still, as Lori had suggested, few people knew what chai was. Our advisory board suggested we hire another ad agency, one with more experience specifically in the beverage industry.

Dwight, our new sales consultant, knew the owner of an ad agency located in San Francisco that boasted relevant heavy hitter clients including Nestle, Lipton and Carnation. This agency fully understood the beverage market with a specific emphasis on tea. But could we attract the owner of such a distinguished firm?

Joel Lewis seemed to be "the" guy for us. He was willing to invest in our company "minus due diligence." At our first meeting, Joel showed us his company's brochure and explained the importance and advantages of hiring an ad agency. We were dazzled by samples of his designers' work. We all believed his agency could do amazing things for us. Our finance consultant was especially awed and urged that we hire them on the spot. Heather and Brian also seemed impressed and suggested moving forward with them, too. But I remained my ever-cautious self so Joel suggested they prepare a proposal for our board of directors and advisory board's consideration. During their subsequent presentation, we were told their fee would amount to about ten percent of our sales. The offer sounded reasonable, their work was first-rate and we were all satisfied. We signed on the dotted line.

We paid Lewis & Partners a retainer and they started work. Joel told us, "Our people loved to work on the (Oregon Chai) business even though it was not a major account, it was a break from the 'know it all approach' of Nestle." They designed four-color counter cards and table tents printed on glossy paper and helped us create a marketing plan. After sampling our original concentrate, they said Oregon Chai tasted heavenly and, since chai originated in India, they conceived of the brilliant tag line: "Nirvana, now available by the cup." But when I saw the image on the proof, I thought the photo of our chai looked strangely like mushroom soup. I voiced this concern to zero response.

I was vindicated when we started getting calls from our customers trying to place orders for the chai dip in the picture.

Not only was the picture confusing but the cost of these new marketing materials the agency designed were considerably higher than I'd anticipated. Covering the ten percent fee necessitated by our agency required that our sales reach increasingly higher levels. We hadn't made such generous sales projections so that ten percent resulted in a substantial sum of money.

It made our argument over our initial twenty-five hundred dollar marketing investment feel like a steal. Despite what I considered to be exorbitant fees, the new agency did have terrific ideas and customers often commented on the quality of our marketing materials. Retailers everywhere were especially pleased with the Oregon Chai POP (point of purchase) program.

Even though I was now principally involved with production, I tried contributing toward these marketing efforts as well. I suggested we affix "Suite T" to our street address, considering it a subtle reminder to anyone who read our address or sent us correspondence that Oregon Chai was a tea. I was gleefully surprised when, sans any snickers, "Suite T" was embraced by all to the extent that it found its way onto our company stationery and all our business cards.

Initially the five founders served as our corporate board of directors, but our attorney advised us that we should place "outsiders" on the board. He felt we needed directors with more experience driving a rapidly growing company. Consequently, we invited some of our advisory board members to become members of the board.

Once the process was completed, our board was then too large. It was suggested that a couple of our original founders resign. I was concerned that whoever was voted off would become terribly upset. But despite my fears, everyone seemed fine with the decision. In the end, Heather, Brian and I were the only members of the original founders remaining on the new Oregon Chai board.

CHAPTER 18

*Another *$#@*! "Learning" Experience!*

With everything happening on a grander scale, I now ordered honey by the truckload - about ten totes - or the equivalent of twenty thousand pounds. One day our honey supplier phoned.

"We've just purchased a large amount of honey at a much lower price," the representative offered. "We'd love to pass that savings on to you."

"How is that possible?" I asked. "What kind of honey is it?"

"It's acacia honey," he said.

"I've never heard of it. What is acacia honey?" I asked.

"It comes from China," he said.

"Oh, no,.." I said, my stomach churning at the mere mention of my nemesis.

"No, thank you!" I managed to grunt.

I'd been down that road before and risking another inferior batch like the one we'd encountered when we first started had less than zero appeal - I didn't care if he gave it to me free! I ordered my normal domestic clover honey.

We scheduled a ten thousand gallon brewing of chai for March 5, 1996. When it came time for manufacturing, all of our ingredients arrived as scheduled. After the chai was brewed, safely transferred to the tankers and sent on its way to the co-packers, I left for home.

As I walked in the door that evening at about seven p.m. the phone was ringing off the hook. It was the plant manager - panicked.

"Something's wrong with the chai," he said.

I rushed back immediately. The lab kept samples of the concentrate in vials and our exquisite brown chai, the batch I had tasted and approved just hours earlier, smelled dreadful - and was turning a greenish-black color. Not again. The honey! I thought. It's the honey again! I called our supplier immediately.

"The person who processed the honey thought it wouldn't make any difference," the receptionist said. "It's just chai."

As it turned out, the supplier had intentionally done an unethical bait and switch. Even though I had flat out refused their "special deal" on the cheap honey - adamantly - they had tried to sneak the "cheap" honey past us thinking no one would be the wiser. How would we ever know? They wagered. 10,000 gallons gone bad, that's how we'd know! I didn't know what to do. It was too late. Again. I was furious.

Some of the lab employees at the manufacturing plant thought the chai didn't taste too bad. Others thought we could sell it since; after all, people mixed it with different things. Some used whole milk, some used non-fat. Others used soymilk or even lemonade.

"It's not the best chai we've ever made," advised one worker. "But it may not be bad enough to toss."

I didn't know what I should do. I called all my partners but couldn't reach anyone. I then called our financial consultant and asked if he had any advice.

"Have twelve people taste the chai," he said, "and ask them how they like it. Don't tell them there's anything wrong with it."

"Okay," I said, tentatively.

I called my son and asked him if he'd come over to my house and bring along a few friends. While I was waiting for them, I plunked down on the couch, leaned over and buried my face in my hands and tried to cry - but no tears would come. I felt like if I could throw up or something, maybe I'd feel better - but nothing. I just sat there, fuming, like a stick of dynamite, ready to blow - but there was no release for the tension, just the vague hope that it would pass with time.

Soon Sean arrived, his friends in tow. We stood around in the kitchen sipping the chai.

"What do you think?" I asked after a few minutes.

They continued sipping.

"It's not bad," they said at first.

But "not bad" wasn't "the best chai in the world." That didn't jive with our mission statement. That wasn't what our Oregon Chai customers had come to expect.

I was afraid Sean's friends were just trying to be kind. But I needed the truth. I needed to hear what they really thought. We chatted awhile longer. I asked again, more assertively.

"Well, I don't really like it," most finally confessed.

In total, there were a couple of people at the plant who said the chai was okay and my son and his friends who said it "wasn't bad." But still, I thought, if we distribute an inferior product, we may upset our loyal customers. And if new customers try it and don't like it, they'll never buy it again. It takes so much marketing and advertising effort to get a customer just to try a new product in the first place, that the last thing we want to do is to lose them due to an erroneous inferior batch. Timing's everything. Not to mention alienating our regular customers for not delivering consistent quality. Losing customers - pre-existing or new - could result in a huge long-term financial loss.

On the other hand, we desperately needed this batch. To make the most of our cash flow I'd been practicing "just in time inventory," a constant balancing act grabbing money the second it came in from sales to cover expenses going out the door for supplies. I sometimes felt as if there was only one dollar - and it was moving as fast as it could.

We had enough chai to fulfill one week's worth of orders. What about the new orders we received? Would we be able to produce enough fast enough if we poured 10,000 gallons down the drain? Probably not.

This presented yet another problem. I didn't want customers believing we were flaky or undependable but the most crucial issue really was our commitment to a superior, consistent quality - and that meant great taste. I decided that this batch of chai didn't stand up to our mission statement to make the best chai in the world.

I asked David what he thought and he said, "Dump it!"

I agreed. So the final, grueling decision was made: to throw out the entire ten thousand gallons of concentrate.

I knew it would cost us financially. But I also knew in my heart it was the right decision. Of that, at least, I had no doubt.

The next problem was ridding ourselves of the ghastly-tasting stuff. Again.

The municipal dump would not accept it. One of our co-packers suggested jokingly that since the chai was already sitting in the trucks that we just open the bottom of the tanks and have them drive around town until all the chai drained out. Tempting as that was I didn't think the Oregon Department of Transportation would approve.

"I can just picture that scene," I laughed. "A hazard-control team would be out on the highway and the evening news would warn people of an unknown, sticky substance all over the road!"

Making the evening news, at least in this way, was not my goal. After several phone calls, we located a feedlot willing to assist us and we dumped the chai there, making a herd of cattle quite happy.

This mistake cost us nearly forty thousand dollars. As our scope grew so did the scale of our errors. The honey company replaced all the honey at no charge (duh). But that only covered the minimal expense of the honey, not all the other ingredients, labor, trucking or feedlot expense we'd incurred - or the down time in making a new batch.

Our attorney advised us we could sue for the cost of the entire run and more than likely we would win but our legal fees would be more than the cost of the loss, not to mention the emotional energy and focus drain away from our primary business, so we opted against it. But you bet we found a new honey supplier.

We continued looking for any opportunities to show our wares at every major national show. We exhibited at the Fancy Food Show, the Natural Products Show, Coffee Fest, the National Restaurant Show as well as smaller, regional shows. It wasn't long before we'd replaced our economical, muslin curtains with a professional trade booth boasting shelves and oversized banners. No more two square feet for us!

In April of '96, Carla and I attended the Portland Chamber of Commerce Trade show. That morning, I stopped at a local grocery store and purchased about six gallons of fresh milk to blend in as our dairy base. We set up our dispensers: one hot and one cold. We mixed about two gallons each (equal parts) of the fresh milk and the chai concentrate in the dispensers and waited anxiously for attendees to sample our chai.

The first person to try it was a young woman. She took a sip, grimaced and quickly walked away. I immediately tried the chai: Ugh. The milk was sour!

Both batches were ruined. I hadn't even thought to try it. I had bought the milk just that morning and it didn't dawn on me to taste that before mixing it. We had to dump everything and start all over again. I had to race out to another store in the middle of the trade show to buy more milk. We learned yet another lesson. From then on, I always sampled the milk and the chai separately before mixing it and then sampled them again together before we gave any tastes out to customers. Let's not talk about what this does to the waistline!

In May of 1996, one of our distributors invited Carla and I to assist at their display at an Associated Grocer's Trade Show. Besides selling our Oregon Chai, they were also marketing cheese so they asked that we wear large, foam-rubber cheese wedges on our heads. Since both of us welcomed a good joke, at first we found it amusing to play along as cheese heads, but it wasn't long before the hats became warm and uncomfortable.

Though Carla was a real sport, I couldn't take the cheddar cap any longer. Unfortunately, my hairdo underneath was a wreck, sweaty strands hung limply around my face. Despite my ruined hair day, Carla and I kept our spirits up and enjoyed the show, laughing and chatting with potential customers.

Still fairly new to the industry and their trade show marketplace and never having worked this particular show before, we weren't aware of all its rules. One policy we were not aware of insisted that a vendor not approach another distributor's customer. A patron approached me and began asking about Oregon Chai. I answered as many questions as possible and then referred him to our distributor's sales representative. After their discussion, she came over to me all keyed up.

"That man is a substantial customer of one of our competitors," she said. "I could not have solicited his business had he not approached you!" She was elated. So was I.

Shortly after this event, Brian found a great new device, a "whipper." It allowed us to mix and serve chai at trade shows and dispensed a frothy, creamy chai latte that looked like it had just been prepared by a professional barista.

I enjoyed both traveling and helping our company's expansion by offering samples to potential customers. In the summer of 1996, I conducted several demonstrations around the Northwest. The summer was our slowest sales time of the year so I didn't have to produce quite as much chai concentrate as normal and was feeling a bit under-utilized. Performing demos provided me with much-needed activity, purpose and contribution - and I loved it.

In the frigid air at six o'clock in the morning, I stood outside an espresso stand in Auburn, Washington, handing samples out to customers as they drove up to grab their morning caffeine. The barista amazed me. She'd see a car approaching and immediately start preparing the customer's favorite non-fat caramel/vanilla latte with three shots of espresso and have it ready and waiting as the car barely slowed to grab it, pay the bill and leave a hefty tip. It was more than obvious that her customer service had earned her a loyal and generous tipping clientele.

On another occasion at a large supermarket, I was asked to set up my demo stand in the wine section of the store. It was a slow morning so I had plenty of time to wander about the aisles, becoming well-acquainted with the many Oregon and Washington wines. I'd had no idea there were so many local vintners, some scoring very high on the Wine Spectator rating.

During this time, I learned that our marketing was significantly more aggressive than the majority of other chai companies. We offered professional-looking four-color, point-of-sale materials including brightly-colored blue and yellow Oregon Chai stickers for the entrance or store window. I never observed marketing materials for any of our competitors. One particular distributor, based in San Francisco, found himself drawn toward Oregon Chai partially as a result of our marketing package.

"I like the way they put their program and packaging together," he said in an interview with Inc. Magazine. "Their competitors are not as professionally handled - a bunch of folks stuck in the '60s."

I finally realized the high cost of marketing and working with ad agencies was well worth the investment. It gave us an edge that set us apart from the competition and truly helped us to succeed. I was thankful to be surrounded by visionaries.

When we required further management experience, we found the perfect candidate, Rex Bird. From an article in The Oregonian, we learned that Rex had recently resigned as president of a local restaurant chain. He was well-respected, had grown the chain considerably and taken it public. Just the skills we needed. Heather said, "We've got to get this guy." We mustered up the courage to call him and asked if he would be willing to help us. Initially, he declined, explaining that it would probably be enjoyable, but Oregon Chai, Inc. was simply not big enough. Upon hearing this I thought I might burst into tears. I was tired and frustrated. The company was growing faster than anyone could imagine, we had a tiger by the tail. There were so many details that needed attention, and I wasn't sure where we needed to go next. I had previous management experience but had never worked with a budget over a million dollars; we needed someone who could see the whole picture and prioritize. So I said, "Rex, I really need your help. Please help me. Please help my daughter. I just can't do it anymore." Rex was quiet while he thought for a minute then finally said he would try to make the time. Again, he thought working with us would be a lot of fun; he certainly felt he could make a contribution, and he loved our product. There was no way we could pay Rex the going rate for someone of his caliber, so we offered him stock options at a discounted rate. This would result in further dilution for the founders but at the time, we could see no other alternative. Rex told us he would join our team, on a part-time basis, but only as chairman of the board of directors - my position.

This was a particularly arduous decision for me. Rex had considerably more experience running a rapidly growing business than I, but I wasn't ready to step down. This company meant everything to me. Heather and I had built Oregon Chai from the ground up, literally, there were chai spices all over my yard! I had been here from Day One. But still, I didn't want to stand in the way of the company's growth by limiting it to the scope of my knowledge and expertise.

I had to admit that Heather and I didn't always communicate perfectly. There is a fine balance between parenting, coaching, running a company and being a business partner. It was truly one of the greatest pleasures of my life to be able to work with and watch my daughter as she grew into a talented executive. However, I was still her mother, so putting a new person as the authority figure or in the position of power on the board would serve all of us. It would certainly take some pressure off me. Each of us needed to focus on our own area of expertise and mine was now most certainly production. I no longer had the time and certainly not the experience to concern myself with every aspect of a fast growing company. The lien on my home had been paid off. That was, after all, the main reason I'd been appointed board chair. We were beyond that now.

After several grueling days, I relented and gave up my chairmanship. But I remained on the board, which now seated six members including Heather, Brian, and three "outsiders." My strategy for Heather to heed the new leadership did work. For a while. Laughably, for a very short while!

As Board Chair, Rex set the agenda for all board meetings, and focused on long-range planning. He looked at sales, distribution and profit margins. He said we needed to bring our cost-of-goods down and in order for us to be profitable we needed to reduce our expenses. Everyone was asked to take a pay cut, to make the company more profitable, to raise its value. Hadn't we just started getting paychecks? Finally? But he argued his mantra that I could repeat in my sleep: "Every reduction in expenses results in an increase of a multiple of twenty to a company's value." In order words, a reduction of say, eight thousand in expenses could increase a company's worth up to one hundred and sixty thousand dollars.

Rex also set up an executive committee with Brian and me as members to consider strategic, long-range planning. We met weekly, usually off-site so we could plan without interruption.

He scheduled workshops with team-building exercises. In one he told us the parable of the "saw." In the story two sawyers are competing. One stops frequently to sharpen his saw while the other frantically saws away, grabbing logs, sawing, tossing the cut pieces to the side, and hurriedly wiping sweat from his brow as the teeth of his blade becomes increasingly dull. Of course, the sawyer who takes time out to occasionally maintain his tool ends up the winner. As Rex said, "If you don't take time out to sharpen your saw, you can't cut as much wood." He also had us do various exercises. One was a test to determine our personality types. The result of mine showed I was an off-the-chart control freak!

On another occasion Rex invited a friend of his who was the CEO of a national company to meet with us. We spent the day learning about business. One of my favorite lessons from this workshop was how to tell if you are maximizing your product's potential. He showed us a bell curve. He said, "Do you know where your product fits on this curve? Ideally you want it at the very top." I found that concept fascinating. We could use the bell-curve to test for the various attributes of our product. For instance, was the level of sweetness right at the top or to one side, being too sweet, or on the other side, not sweet enough? Using this method we would learn what our consumers wanted and maximize sales.

It wasn't long before George, our ever vigilant attorney, advised that we add one more member to our board of directors.

"It's better to have an odd number of board members," he explained, "just in case you have a tie vote."

Dwight and Joel began actively seeking the recruitment of one of their friends into our company. Mike Wigell offered numerous years of experience with trade journals and trade shows and held extensive knowledge about product branding. We invited him to join the board.

He agreed. We discovered that not only was he an experienced businessman with significant contacts, but he always maintained a Cheshire-cat smile, helping cheer up our sometimes dreary office whenever he visited town, especially on all-to-frequent, rainy Portland afternoons.

We did out best to convince customers that Oregon Chai was delicious hot or cold. However, in spite of our efforts, the perception was of a warm drink and the company experienced some seasonality in sales. Because summer was such a slow time of year for Oregon Chai, Heather chose this time to marry her fiancé, David Howitt. (Yes, she married a man with her father's name - we both married Davids).

All of our money had been used to finance the company. When we started planning the wedding, my likewise ever-frugal husband suggested a "potluck." Now, a potluck can be fun, and it certainly is a reasonable solution when you have a modest budget, but that is not most brides' fantasy and it certainly wasn't Heather's. She broke down in tears. Not only was she under the same incredible stress that I was, but she was a bride during all of this. I was just dealing with menopause.

I turned to my husband and suggested he find something else to do. Heather and I would work out the details. That afternoon I rented him a copy of "Father of the Bride," the one starring Spencer Tracy. This seemed to give him a more reasonable perspective. Once he was out of the picture, Heather and I set about working out all the details and as far as I was concerned she would have the wedding of her dreams, even if it meant I had to refinance my house - and it did.

I was really proud of many of the decisions she made. Instead of expecting her ten bridesmaids to go to the expense of purchasing gowns that they may never wear again, she asked each one to wear her favorite, classic "little black dress" that they all inevitably already owned or would happily update.

For herself, Heather found a lovely, simple white gown right off the rack. It was more of a long cocktail dress as opposed to a bridal gown - one she could easily use in the future.

She booked the wedding for an afternoon at the Shakespeare Garden in the City of Portland's famous rose garden. Luckily the rain held off until everyone left for the reception which was held at the Portland Racquet Club, a stone craftsman's style building similar to those built following the depression under the Federal Works Progress Administration. There, our guests enjoyed a buffet of delicious food. I think I ate one grilled asparagus spear the whole evening.

Heather also hired a local band: Pink Martini. With my Associates Degree in Music, I had done a little professional singing in my former life. The leader of the band asked me if I would like to prepare a song to sing. No way. The last thing I needed as Mother of the Bride was to worry about performing!

But there was magic in the air. Towards the end of the evening, feeling relieved that everything had gone off so well and that Heather was as happy as I could possibly wish, the conductor asked me again if I would like to join them. I said, "Sure," and much to my surprise, probably gave one of the best performances of my life. What a way to go out!

And for one precious night, I didn't dream about being washed away in a flood of warm, sweet chai and I didn't worry about what new lessons I may learn or barriers I might be forced to overcome - my little girl just got married.

.

Heather working in the office, 1995

Brian handing out Oregon Chai at a
Grateful Dead concert, 1995

4   March 8, 1995   NEWS   Daily Vanguard

PSU grad brings Himalayan tea to Oregon

The spicy answer to lattes is gaining momentum

ANGELA POTTER
Vanguard Staff

PSU graduate student Heather McMillen was traveling through the Himalayas when she was struck with a burning desire for a latté. But lattés were nowhere to be found. Instead, she found chai, an ancient tea that included a potpourri of spices mixed with hot steamy milk.

When she returned to the United States, her craving for chai led McMillen to open her own business on a shoestring with her mother, PSU student Tedde McMillen, as her business partner.

Tedde applied for a business license after getting tired of hearing her daughter complain of the hundredth time about wanting to start her own business making chai, Heather McMillen said.

On July 28, 1992, Broadway Bakery became the first place to sell Oregon Chai. Next was the Meetro. After that, Nature's picked up the product.

"Now we're in over a hundred places," McMillen said.

Oregon Chai's success is not just local. The budding company is about to start selling their product all over the country.

"We're basically about to go nationwide. One of our distributors has over 4,000 accounts throughout Oregon and throughout the West Coast. We're ready to move outward," said Brian Ross, Oregon Chai's chief operating officer.

The milky drink is guaranteed to give you as much zing as any caffeinated tea, maybe more. Ross said chai is not buzz-free because it's made from black tea and honey.

"The honey, because it's so sweet, and the caffeine combined gets people really buzzed. It's a sugar—caffeine high," Ross said.

Chai also has soothing elements such as vanilla and ginger.

McMillen's discovery of chai in the Himalayas was purely accidental.

"Basically, it's everywhere (in Asia). I didn't notice it at first," she said.

But once she discovered an old man selling it on the street, McMillen said she would drink literally "twenty cups a day." Every one who has had it may like it made a little bit differently, McMillen said.

"It's like chocolate chip cookies. There are a thousand different recipes. Ours is much more Americanized — lots of vanilla, really sweet, like a latté," she said.

Although McMillen couldn't find it anywhere in Portland, she later discovered chai in Santa Cruz and became even more of an addict.

Even though Oregon Chai is a booming success, the McMillens and crew are still on a tight budget for their own living expenses. Any profits at this point are being redistributed within the company, Ross said.

"We want to put all the money that we make back into the company to buy more ingredients," Ross said.

McMillen admits that with the financial hardship of a new business she still eats every meal at her parents and lives off of her boyfriend.

"Right now we're really poor. We're working so hard and we know things are going well so we're able to not stress. We have a really good support network," Ross said.

Mother and daughter admit they make good business partners.

"It works. Because if your mom gets mad at you, it doesn't matter because it's just your mom," McMillen said.

Tedde is a general studies major with ambitions to continue her efforts in Oregon Chai.

"It's so important for everyone to have an education. In any field that you go into, it broadens you as a person, makes you capable of critical thinking, and carrying on a staff meeting or dealing with confrontation," Tedde McMillen said.

Heather McMillen (left) and Brian Ross have been busy promoting their company's new hot drink offering, Oregon Chai. The free samples passed out in Smith Center met with mostly favorable reviews.

VanguardPHIL KINDSCHUH

Article in the Daily Vanguard, 1995

Tea Invades Coffee Country

By SUSAN G. HAUSER

Article in The Wall Street Journal, 1995

Nirvana in a Cup: The founding of Oregon Chai   211

Carla, her daughter Liette and Tedde's nephew Eric brewing
chai at Oregon State University, summer, 1995

Tedde loading a cart with finished product after a day
of production at OSU, 1995

Oregon Chai marketing material, 1995

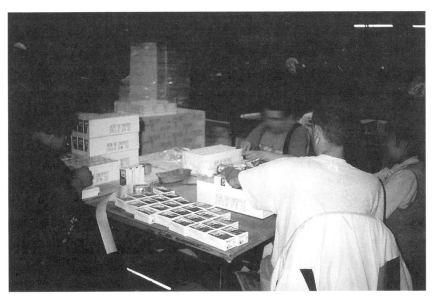

Workers at ProPaking, a division of CCI Enterprises.
Milwaukie, Oregon, 1995

DAVID K. BERKWITZ—NEWSWEEK
Hotter than a latte: *How to sip a cookie*

Hot Cha Cha, Hot Cha Chai

Food: Out West, coffee breaks mean it's teatime

IN SANTA CRUZ, BOULDER AND OTHER trend-setting spots in the West, fancy coffees have been on tap for so long that the mention of a blueberry vanilla latte provokes only a yawn. So coffee-bar regulars are ordering *chai*—hot or iced. Inspired by the hot, milky tea available in India ("chai" means "tea" in Hindi and Russian), the American version is a tea fragrant with cardamom, cinnamon and other spices. "Chai has been a very arcane beverage until recently," says Elizabeth Bertani, director of marketing at LiveChai in Boulder. "But the specialty-tea trend is following right behind specialty coffees."

Heather McMillen first tasted chai in India. Last year she and her mother went into business in Portland, Ore., and now sell about 2,000 gallons of Oregon Chai concentrate a month, mostly in the West but increasingly to cafés in the East. This month Oregon Chai, like LiveChai, will become available in aseptic packaging—juice-box style, with a straw. Unlike some of the other chais, Oregon Chai has little tea flavor. "Our chai is really dessert-y," says McMillen. She's right: drinking it is a bit like sipping spice cookies. "That's part of the appeal," says Matt Kuhn of Someday Cafe in Somerville, Mass. "It's a sweet drink that isn't a soda pop or a Snapple." If other brands follow suit, chai could take off. After all, it wasn't coffee that made Starbucks a national mania—it was milk, sugar, cream and chocolate.   LAURA SHAPIRO

Article in Newsweek, 1995

Nirvana in a Cup: The founding of Oregon Chai

Brian Ross and Heather in Oregon chai's first trade show
booth at NASCORE, 1995

1,500 gallons of Oregon Chai brewing at manufacturer, 1995

Carla observing aseptic process as part of
our R & D program, 1996

Marketing material featuring new tagline,
"Nirvana. Now available by the cup.", 1996

SECTION IV:

Sweeten The Pot

CHAPTER 19

A Truckload of Ca$h

The receptionist interrupted me during a board meeting at our attorney's office.

"Tedde," she whispered, "you have an important call. It's urgent."

I left the meeting at once and grabbed the receiver. Our co-packer was on the line.

"The tanker with your product hasn't arrived," he said. "Do you know where it is?"

We'd finished filling the truck the evening before and the tanker had departed at midnight. The truck was scheduled for arrival at the co-packers for unloading by five o'clock that morning. Where was it?

"I know the truck left," I said, "because I was there."

Beads of perspiration formed on my eyelids, my upper lip trembled.

Where on earth could the tanker be? He was several hours late. But no word? At all?

"I'll call the manufacturer," I said, "and call you right back."

To our benefit, our manufacturer made all the arrangements for the tankers, meaning the responsibility for the tanker lay with them, not with me. Still, where was our chai? I phoned them immediately.

"I'll call the trucking company and try to find that tanker," a representative for our manufacturer said.

I prayed they'd find it. I called the co-packer back.

"We're searching for the tanker," I said.

"Well, okay, but we'll have to charge you for the cost of the plant's downtime," he said.

"But that's not our fault," I said. "The tanker left on time."

"It's still your responsibility," he insisted. "You booked the time and we've held it for you. The crew arrived as scheduled and now they're just milling around. It's been about four hours."

I tried negotiating with him but there was nothing I could do.

"Okay," I said finally. "We'll pay for the time."

An hour later, our manufacturer finally located the tanker. As it turned out, the driver was so weary that he'd pulled over alongside the road to rest. Unfortunately for us all, he'd overslept and missed his delivery deadline. When he did finally turn up, the chai was packaged safely and we were back in business. Luckily for us, and rightly so, the trucking company, rather than Oregon Chai, paid the plant for their downtime. From that moment on, we advised the trucking company that the tankers must arrive on time - or they would be held liable for the downtime fines. Our co-packer owned a couple of refrigerated holding tanks, so our chai could arrive a day in advance if necessary. But no matter how hard we tried or how much we warned otherwise, every now and then a driver missed a delivery time.

One particular delivery was skipped mid-summer, in the middle of unusually warm temperatures. We'd always cooled the chai concentrate before pumping it into the tanker. But I was distressed, concerned that the chai would get too warm and spoil. I phoned the company at once.

"It will lose about one degree Fahrenheit over a twenty-four hour period," they said.

But I was not appeased. Not after all the safety and storage hoops we'd jumped through.

"You tell that driver to take his tanker up the nearest mountain. If he's going to sleep, you tell him to park it in the snow under a tree!"

The drivers also tried to cram as much as possible into their trucks. Sometimes they would stack the pallets two high, one on top of the other, which would simply collapse in on itself as our cardboard packaging wasn't designed to support that much weight. The pallets would fall over and cases were smashed. The containers would split open and the sweet, sticky chai would drench the inside of their trailer.

We asked the warehouse owner to stop stacking the pallets this high and warned them to only pack one layer in the trailers. But it didn't help. I finally created signs for each pallet that read "Do Not Top Load." We'd slap one of these on each side after the pallets were wrapped in cellophane. This seemed to resolve the issue.

All the trucking problems aside, after working with drivers of both tankers and semis, I came to realize that truckers represent the last remnant of the free-spirited American West. They are truly the last American cowboys. They do what they want, when they want - a quality I find admirable in a world packed with so much hyperactivity and begrudging submission to social mores. Still, I was always thankful when a delivery arrived at its destination. And if it arrived on schedule or before, I praised God - and truckers - for yet another miracle.

Carla took over the complex trucking arrangements. She obtained prices through a trucking broker, scheduled trucks for pickup at the warehouse, prepared the bills of lading (a legal document that gives the warehouse permission to release our product to a third party) and made certain our chai was stocked and ready to go.

Carla was so well organized that the whole system ran smoothly. The truckers and dispatch operators all enjoyed her warm and friendly manner. She fully understood the complexities of the shipping industry, such as product codes and pallet configurations - aspects of the industry I knew next to nothing about. Carla knew all of our brokers by first name and was always chatting and laughing as she scheduled pickups and delivery of our chai.

Once on the road and delivered, it was Heather and the sales team's responsibility to take over and make certain the chai was properly positioned in the store. Effective displays and adequate advertisement including either shelf talkers, signs on the counters or Oregon Chai stickers at the retailers' entrance were our primary emphases. It required more than simply delivering our chai to compel a sale but between our distribution and marketing powerhouse, our customers couldn't resist.

More and more distributors were contacting us. We would never sign another exclusive agreement again. We didn't need to. That was now their issue. If they wanted to carry our top-selling and in-demand product, we'd let the free market decide who and how Oregon Chai was distributed. We let them sort out their own territories and customers. We offered volume pricing, so the more Oregon Chai concentrate they purchased, the better their pricing became.

We greatly appreciated the help of our consultants, yet it was often difficult to give up control of the company we had worked so hard to build. At one point we were even asked to take a pay cut! We had always focused on growing sales and maintaining a consistently high quality product. It seemed like they were myopically focused on the bottom line.

During one particularly memorable board meeting, Rex suggested we each figure out what we wished to attain from our experience with Oregon Chai - and how we perceived it ending.

At some future point, he suggested hypothetically, would we consider selling our company? Would we consider taking it public?

I couldn't imagine my life without Oregon Chai. I had little desire to leave the company and going public would result in increased scrutiny and additional paperwork. I certainly didn't need anymore of that!

Despite all these concerns, I knew it was probably in my best interests to at least walk through the exercise of an exit strategy. Pencil it out. I should think about how much money I would need upon my departure. I received a small pension from my many years working as a public employee but my husband, as a self-employed architect, had none.

Taking this into consideration, I estimated what I would need to live comfortably until the age of ninety, give or take. I based my projected amount on a fairly modest price per share. It seemed workable, so, fine: there, I had my plan.

A few weeks later, I was asked to sell some of my shares to attract investors with more experience.

It was ironic that had I not done as Rex asked in developing an exit strategy and calculating what I would need in order to sell my stock, I wouldn't have known what I was holding on to - or why. I had done exactly what he asked and I figured out I couldn't sell any of my stock. It had already been diluted plenty. Weren't there enough corporate shares still available? Why did they have to be mine?

As our company expanded, each of its founders experienced similar requests. None sold out. We had been successful in figuring out how to start our company and, although we'd made our share of mistakes, we'd also made plenty of competent decisions, day after day after very long day. We were the ones who had made it grow and prosper.

Each integral stage of our rapidly expanding enterprise required new, more advanced skills - and we had each risen to the occasion. Sometimes we learned within our experiences, adapting just enough to resolve the issue ourselves. Other times, we required the knowledge of outside consultants. If they weren't sufficient, we hired the necessary experts.

Our accounting department was the first one that got overhauled. Carla did an adequate job, but she had no accounting background and was therefore unable to create balance sheets or profit and loss statements. So we placed an ad in the local paper for an accountant. Once hired, Carla would manage the accounting department, helping hire accounts receivable and accounts payable clerks but eventually she left accounting and mainly handled the company's complex shipping needs.

On January 8, 1997, several weeks after Heather's final meeting with Starbucks, Lori composed a press release announcing "Oregon Chai, Inc. Hits the Million Dollar Mark," representing a sales increase over the prior year of 420%.

In the release, Heather stated that the sales surge reflected Oregon Chai's "great tasting product with attractive packaging, exciting point of sale program, excellent word of mouth and loyal customers," while Brian, now Oregon Chai's Chief Operating Officer, suggested that the "increase in sales was primarily due to the increase of distributors and the addition of large chain accounts such as Seattle's Best Coffee, Gloria Jean's Gourmet Coffee and Nordstrom."

He added that "we believe we are positioning Oregon Chai as the market leader." But I liked the straightforward words of the President of the Texas Restaurant Association: "This stuff rocks."

I believed the reason for our phenomenal growth was simpler: people just loved our chai.

Maintaining our brisk sales meant keeping our sales team on the go, twenty-four hours a day. Heather and Brian created estimates for the entire year, projecting $1.8 million in sales, so in truth, they were disappointed - as were our consultants, that we had only hit $963,984 for 1996 - just shy of a million dollars - but a 420% growth rate was nothing to sneeze at. I was pretty darn happy hitting the million-dollar mark. I had felt all the growth pains and I don't know how we could've grown much faster (without a bucket load of cash and a fleet of therapists!)

When we hired our first full-time employee, Kurt Peterson, a CPA, as our accountant, to our dismay, he discovered that our price did not cover the cost of brokers, the various discounts we offered or the types of fees a company begins to incur when selling in larger volumes - which was all new territory to us.

He crafted a complex model that lead with the cost of goods sold, followed by the markup for sales discounts with terms of a two percent discount if the invoice was paid in less than ten days but the total amount due within thirty days (referred to as 2% 10, net 30), returns allowance, demo allowance, inbound receipt, order picking, handling in and out at our warehouse (if the warehouse ships less than a full pallet, charges would be per case for all cases they handled).

He also calculated the in-warehouse storage, the warehouse order charge, the co-packer's transportation to the warehouse, the five percent broker commissions, two percent for other commissions, pallet costs and insurance for the total freight on board (product loaded on the truck) and our warehouse cost. His hope was to achieve a ten percent net profit margin after-taxes.

Quite simply, we needed a price that covered all of our expenses and left us with a satisfactory profit. A single case, shipped by a common carrier, was the most expensive. An entire truckload (about twenty pallets filled with seventy-five cases each) obviously cost the least.

So, in order to increase our sales and profits in keeping with our new accountant's suggestions, we restructured our pricing along his model, providing our customers with greater incentives for volume purchasing.

Lori assembled pricing sheets listing everything a potential customer must know before placing an order: pack/size, how many quarts to a case, an easily scannable UPC code for each product, price (our customers took ownership of the chai when they picked it up and paid shipping themselves), case dimensions for ease of in-warehouse storage and case weight (so trucks could calculate their weights to stay within regulations and avoid fines).

Lori also included pallet dimensions for planning layout in respective trucker's trailers, type of packaging (quarts and 1.5-gallon), date of manufacturing and the use-by or sale date that determined the chai's shelf life.

Sales were getting increasingly complex. One day as I sat in my office, sipping on iced chai, I received a questionnaire. As I tore it open, I noted the name of one of our distributors on the letterhead. I glanced over the litany of information it requested.

What regulations applied to Oregon Chai, it asked: CFR, NLEA, OFPA, or DSHEA?

I hadn't the vaguest notion of what any of these acronyms meant.

"How am I going to fill this out?" I asked myself out loud, dumbfounded.

But that wasn't all the questionnaire asked. It asked for answers to questions that I considered proprietary. How could I answer these without giving away any of our secrets?

Aside from sharing confidential information, I was even more concerned that if I filled out the form incorrectly, the distributor might then be unwilling to handle our product.

I asked around, wondering if anyone could assist me, but no one else at Oregon Chai knew how to fill the form out either - or had any idea what it was all about. I agonized over it for days, reading each question over and over, wondering what to do? What would happen if I didn't fill it out? Finally, I just dove in and started jotting down answers.

Who owns your company? That's an easy one, I thought, we do.

Do you adhere to a specific industry code of ethics? Yes, or no? If yes, please attach a copy. I enclosed our mission statement. What else could they want?

List any industry trade groups to which your company belongs. I wandered around our office asking if anyone was associated with any trade groups. Then I remembered that I'd joined IFT, the local food technologists association so that I could attend their meetings. We had also joined the Specialty Coffee Association of America. I scribbled them both down.

The questionnaire went on.

What government permits or licenses does your company hold? We currently held a processor's license as well as a federal identification number. I noted them both.

What regulations are you required to comply with? Other than not placing hot, steaming chai into a cold glass bottle (I'd learned that the hard way), we really had no specific regulations. Once our kitchen was approved, we were left virtually on our own. We'd heard nothing from the F.D.A. about our label, so we figured it must be okay. I answered the question to the best of my knowledge and in the most general of terms.

Is your facility open for visitors? Nope.

Do you own or operate a manufacturing facility? Are you kidding? I giggled. I'm lucky to operate my gas stove!

Are your products manufactured by other companies? Another easy one. Yes, but it's a secret.

I was midway through the form, feeling more confident that I could actually fill it out properly. This isn't so bad after all, I thought. But the questions got harder.

What procedures or programs do you use to ensure quality control in the manufacturing process? I wondered if they'd be happy to know that I tasted every batch - and had the extra twenty pounds to prove it.

How have your personnel been trained? The school of hard knocks, taste and smell.

Are raw materials tested for quality when received? Finally, one I could answer with conviction. Yes, I wrote, I always make a batch of chai whenever I receive a new shipment of raw ingredients.

I moved on to the next question.

What type of record keeping is used to ensure an audit trail for the product and its ingredients? Ah, you've come to the right person, I thought. I had tables and charts for every single batch. I'd kept so many records, it drove our accountant crazy. Thank goodness for Microsoft Excel. I made a note on the form.

Do you batch test? Yes, I wrote, every time.

Are batch or lot samples retained? If so, for how long? Yes, we keep samples, I noted. We don't have a standard amount of time for holding onto samples, but we have a bit from every batch, starting with our very first one.

I wrote and wrote, then wrote some more. I wrote until my hand ached. Then I read slowly over each answer, until I was confident it was as complete as I could make it. Then I faxed the form to the distributor and waited for a reply. After several days with no response, I assumed our answers were sufficient. Kind of like the F.D.A. They probably just filed it away, I guessed. But as a consumer myself, I appreciated knowing that our grocery distributors and stores may actually have paid attention to details like the ones I'd provided. A few weeks later, we received a copy of the distributor's quality standards. I looked it over, satisfied that we'd met them all. And they continued dispensing our products.

On January 1, 1997, Seattle's Best Coffee selected Oregon Chai for their nationwide outlets. At that time, they owned forty-five shops, with thirty more planned for construction. Both Oregon Chai and Seattle's Best shared a common value of offering their customers superior quality so being chosen as the chai supplier for this major espresso chain marked a significant step.

In an interview, Seattle's Best's marketing manager stated that "The Oregon Chai product is a good fit for our brand because it maintains a high quality taste profile that our customers really enjoy." We were thrilled.

In February, it was deemed that we needed a cash infusion of about $150,000 to help us keep up with production and not suffer from growth pains. The fastest and most efficient means of securing the funds was to get a credit line secured by the personal guarantees of all the board members. To my utter astonishment, everyone agreed. It dawned on me how much potential this board saw in our little company if they were all uniformly willing to go personally on the line for that much money. We gave them stock options in return for their trust.

We were that close. In March of 1997, the very next month, we became profitable. It took us almost three years and with a great deal of help from Rex and Kurt, Brian drew up a new business plan.

CHAPTER 20

The Rape of the Queen Bee

Our margins needed improving. Our manufacturer suggested we use cane syrup in place of some of the honey. Not that we hadn't had enough honey issues for one company's history, but we did have other fears about honey. A mite that infected the hives of already-endangered wild honeybees was a newsworthy concern that was driving up the price of domestic honey as domestic honeybees were being outsourced to pollinate places abroad. The mite scare caused honey futures to skyrocket as major shortages in the honey supply were predicted. Thus, getting out of the honey market became quite appealing, to say the least.

Still, I refused to alter our formulation unless I was absolutely certain it would not affect the taste or quality of our chai. I researched suppliers and finally located some organic cane syrup and I began testing. Oh the joy of this food science stuff, not music to my ears at all.

We evaluated different ratios of honey to syrup and then offered samples to everyone in our office. When we were satisfied with the final combination of honey and organic cane syrup, we conducted a blind study, where no one knew which product contained the cane syrup. To our amazement: not a single person could tell the difference - not even Heather.

Still, our sales team was nervous, certain that altering our chai would affect sales. But I was reassured by the blind tests and confident that substituting the honey with cane syrup was the right decision. We made the change and didn't receive a single comment from any of our many Oregon Chai consumers. With the addition of the organic cane syrup the product could now be organically certified and by leaving out the honey, we were able to provide a product for vegan chai enthusiasts also. Consequently our new, Oregon Chai Organic concentrate was born.

As our sales increased so did our need for greater chai production.

The more chai concentrate we brewed, the more efficient our manufacturer became. The challenge was our manufacturer could brew more chai than the co-packer could package in a day but our co-packer wouldn't schedule more than one eight-hour shift per day - and we were afraid that they wouldn't be able to keep up with our production potential - which could limit our sales to their capacity. We were concerned that one day in the near future we may be forced to slow or halt production.

This escalating situation made both our new Controller and the Board uneasy. The members shared their concerns, insisting I find another facility, one that wouldn't stymie the growth of our rapidly expanding company. So the search was on for other, more flexible co-packers.

Before long, Oregon Chai began popping up in espresso bars and natural food stores all around the United States. We now had one hundred and thirty distributors nationwide and Oregon Chai was now available in all fifty states in thirty-five hundred locations.

Sometimes, our chai turned up in the oddest places.

I received an email from one of our brokers telling us that his parents were traveling around the country in their Eagle bus. The broker had recently mailed his mother a quart of our Original Chai concentrate. She tried it, loved it, but couldn't find any during her RV trip. While in Blue Earth, Minnesota, his father stopped at Radio Shack needing some parts for their RV's satellite dish. He searched around, up and down each aisle, but couldn't find the items. So, on his way back to the RV, he passed the checkout stand and discovered something the pair needed even more: Radio Shack was selling Oregon Chai.

Many customers didn't know what chai was, so awareness was our biggest obstacle. Whenever I traveled, I always looked for opportunities to introduce people to Oregon Chai. I carried quarts that I could give away. At restaurants, I would grab a business card and ask for the manager's name. Then, when I returned home, I'd send a letter and a sample. I understood that it was risky for a retailer to add it to their menu since Oregon Chai cost more than coffee. But once they started serving chai, many found it well worth the investment, as customers would often come in specifically for that menu item.

I paid attention to the way our chai was prepared and served. I always offered my appreciation for the espresso bars, restaurants, stores and their staffs that served our Oregon Chai. Whenever I observed a barista performing a particularly fine job, I would ask his or her name and write a commendation note to their boss.

One day, my husband and I made a trip to the beach, stopping at a small espresso bar along the way. Oregon Chai was on its menu, so I ordered one. I watched as the barista prepared it. He poured chai into a steaming pitcher, then grabbed some half-n-half from the refrigerator and blended it with the concentrate. I was stunned. I peered at my husband.

"That's so fattening," I said. "I'd better go speak with him."

I didn't always introduce myself when I visited coffee houses, but this was different. I had to let him know he was doing it all wrong. I trotted up to the counter.

"Hi there," I said. "I'm Tedde, the owner of Oregon Chai."

He grinned.

"Hello!"

"I was noticing the way you blend your chai," I said. "We recommend that our customers use whole or two percent milk."

He looked puzzled.

"Oh, no," he insisted, shaking his head. "I talked to Heather and she said I should mix the chai half and half."

I chuckled to myself knowing that Heather meant he should mix it half milk and half Oregon Chai concentrate.

I learned later that this young man had developed a vast, loyal following. Patrons traveled from Portland, praising him for blending the best chai in Oregon. Despite my admonition, it seemed his customers enjoyed the richer taste of the half-n-half. From that point on, in our instructions, we always stated mix equal parts.

On another occasion, during a visit to Java Man, a local Portland espresso bar, I noticed the barista training a new employee.

"You have to be careful not to get the product too hot," I overheard her say. "It's very important because excessive heat can scorch not only the milk, but it can effect the honey as well."

I was happy to learn that this barista expressed such concern for the quality of her chai. A few moments later, she approached and served my chai.

"Would you care for some Mexican chocolate sprinkled on the top?" she asked. "It compliments the spices."

"Oh, I'd love some!" I said. It was excellent.

I was gratified whenever I'd find people taking a genuine interest in our product, paying close attention to detail, in turn providing their customers a better experience. Nearly each time I spoke with one of our customers, I'd discover something new about our chai, a new way of blending it or new things to add. That was so in keeping with chai's heritage.

"Do you know that queen bees are raped?" the caller said on the phone without so much as saying hello.

I thought I'd misheard. Was she talking about bees?

"What did you say?" I asked, confused, setting what I was working on down on my desk.

"Queen Bees are raped in the hive," the caller repeated. "And not only that, beekeepers paint targets on their backs and," she shrieked, "cut their wings."

I winced, imagining the pain of the tiny, defenseless queens as their wings were cut leaving them to be ripped violently apart by the inevitable gang rape that lay waiting hopelessly in their future. The image was horrific. I didn't know what to say. I wondered if the call was a crank. I almost hoped it was so I could hang up and try to shake the image from my head.

But the caller wasn't laughing.

I realized she was serious.

I took a long, cleansing breath. She was an Oregon Chai customer after all and the customer is always right. I wanted her satisfied. I listened carefully, treating her with respect.

"I wasn't aware of all this," I said finally, trying to conclude the conversation. "But I will most certainly discuss the situation with our supplier and get back to you just as soon as I can."

I didn't know what else to say. I just hoped she'd be appeased.

"Thank you," she said, with relief in her voice. "I'll be waiting to hear back."

As promised, I immediately phoned our honey vendor, a man who'd also worked for several years as a beekeeper. I relayed the frantic caller's story.

"What a nut!" he laughed. But as soon as he realized I wasn't laughing along with him, he continued: "Um, beekeepers used to mark the queens, but that practice has long since been abandoned."

"Go on," I urged. I wanted every detail so I could respond to this woman.

"The necessity of clipping the queen's wings was to keep them from flying away," he explained. "It didn't hurt them. It was more like clipping your fingernails."

Since this vendor was an industry professional, I was satisfied that I'd received enough information and that the practice of wing clipping was no longer used. I phoned my customer and told her what I'd just learned.

I also notified her that the Oregon Chai team offered our vegan customers a certified organic chai concentrate that was sweetened with organic cane syrup and contained no honey.

"Thank you so much for calling me back so quickly," she said.

Honey. The bane of my existence.

An important part of the success of any business is customer service and it became a major focus of Oregon Chai. Our goal was to exceed customer's expectations and as a small company, we simply had to outperform everyone else. I knew we must be doing something right: Oregon Chai was the first chai brand formally recognized in the United States, and we were the undisputed leader in a brand new beverage category that we had helped to create.

I searched anywhere I could for tips on making our customer service superior. One afternoon, I read the following story in a book: "Northern Italy today is the richest region of Europe. Reginald Bartholomew, a former American ambassador to Italy, once explained why to me. He said 'Let's say you come to France, Germany and Italy and tell them, "I want to buy some purple cheese." What happens? Well, the French will tell you, 'Monsieur, cheese is never purple.' The Germans will tell you, 'Purple cheese is not in the catalogue this year.' But the Italians...Ah, the Italians will say to you, 'What shade of purple would you like? Magenta?' If northern Italy were a stock, I'd hold it[1]."

As I read through the narrative, it struck me instantly as the perfect customer service metaphor. Luckily, like the Italians, every one on the Oregon Chai team took our customer's comments and concerns seriously, making every effort to accommodate their needs.

---

[1] Thomas L. Friedman, *The Lexus and the Olive Tree*, Waterville, ME, Thorndike Press, 1999, page 347.

C H A P T E R   2 1

Me Write?

A tea importer invited Carla and I to attend a tea conference in upstate New York. We accepted and while there, we met the editor of the Tea & Coffee Trade Journal. We chatted for a while, discussing Oregon Chai and the tea industry. Then she asked if I'd write an article on chai for the magazine.

"We'd be honored to publish your story," she said.

I was excited, but concerned.

"I'd love to," I said. "But I don't know if I'm a good enough writer."

Sour memories emerged. When I was a college freshman, I scored poorly in English Composition. In fact, I did so badly that my instructor, who graded my work a "D" during the first term, demanded that I never return to her class. But since I was working long hours, I registered late and wound up assigned to her class a second time. At our first course meeting, I seated myself in the farthest corner of the room, in hopes she wouldn't notice. But she was a sharp lady. She saw me, leaped up and, in front of the entire class, pointed a long, narrow index finger straight at me.

"Get out of my class!" she demanded.

I was mortified, shrinking into my corner. The whole class just stared at me. My eyes darted back and forth, looking for an exit. Slowly, I rose from my chair and inched myself out the nearest door. From that moment on I worked hard, enrolling in several courses to improve my writing.

"Ok, I'll do it," I said defiantly.

I had never anticipated composing anything for publication but I forged ahead with the project anyhow. It took me several weeks and I was surprised when the journal's editor returned my first draft with just a handful of corrections. She published my article in the July 1997 issue. Oregon Chai not only got me out of my laid off funk - but it launched my writing career.

I loved trade shows. They were like treasure hunts to me. You never knew what you'd find as you surveyed all the new, innovative products. In 1997, just three years after Heather and I had founded Oregon Chai, I attended the National Food Processors' Association convention and trade show. My plan was to search for new product ideas. Our consultants insisted that we expand our offerings of chai flavors.

Our package supplier set up a booth at the show and among their exhibits was an eleven-ounce aseptic container that they were just introducing. It was spherical, like a can, and their sample had a metallic finish, designed to replace the eight-ounce kid's juice box. They were certain that a carton that fit a car's beverage holder would offer widespread adult appeal. I liked the way it looked and I wanted it right away.

"Who packs this container?" I asked.

"Right now we're trying to sell the idea to packers," the representative said. "But I don't know who has the equipment or who's ordering it."

I left the trade show confident I'd found a feasible solution to some of our ready-to-drink packaging problems.

Back home in Portland, I reported my show findings. But my discovery of the new eleven-ounce container received a tepid response. I was disappointed, but that was okay, I just needed to make a better pitch, I rationalized. If they could see the container, ideally plastered with our award-winning graphics, maybe they could envision the future I saw.

I phoned our co-packer.

"Are you set up to process this new container?" I asked eagerly.

But the representative was vague, not really knowing if they were capable of processing it or not.

The following spring, Heather and I met with the co-packer. He still wouldn't divulge whether his company had acquired the equipment for the new container, but he did have packaging prototypes and shared them with Heather and me. But rather than the striking, metallic ones I'd seen in Chicago, his samples were simple, white boxes. Heather was unimpressed. Still, I remained optimistic. I knew they were the way to go.

I attended the National Restaurant Show in Chicago in October. It was amazing how we went from no chai vendors at the first show we attended in February of 1995 to finding several just a couple of years later.

That year there were numerous new chai manufacturers and several instant, powdered chais. Now this makes sense, I told myself. Few small operators own elaborate espresso equipment that can steam our tea lattes but they all can add hot water to a powdered mix. I was convinced that we needed to break into that category, too.

While attending the show, I met with one of our new, large distributors who also envisioned the opportunity for an instant chai. They wanted us to create a dry product capable for use in the convenience store beverage dispensers. I was flattered that they would approach us with product development, but Oregon Chai was not a product development company. If I was going to have to go to all that effort to figure out how to create a powdered chai, we were going to own it. We could license it to them or I was even willing to private label it for them (where it's our product but we put their label on it), but no matter what we did, we would retain ownership.

Unfortunately, the distributor wanted only a recipe - just like Starbucks. When we informed them that Oregon Chai wanted further involvement, they said our differences were irreconcilable and withdrew their support.

A few months later, the distributor developed its own instant chai, offering it at local convenience stores. I tasted some at a store near my home and found it dreadful. I thought this product could wound the chai market leaving those who'd tried it unwilling to taste another. I phoned the buyer at the store's headquarters.

"How are your sales?" I asked.

"Well," he began, "initially the sales for this chai were very good, but there's been no repeat business." (I wonder why.)

"Do you think there's a market for the powdered chai, then?" I asked.

"The initial sales indicate there is a market," he said, "but my customers don't like the chai I'm selling."

This sounded like an opportunity for Oregon Chai to me.

"Are you willing to try another brand?" I asked.

"Certainly," he said.

So I started developing one for us. I tried matching the flavor of our original chai using all natural ingredients but I had a hard time finding a flavorsome cream and finally broke down and used one with some artificial flavors. I rationalized that since our target audience for this product (convenience store customers) was less health conscious, they would probably be more forgiving of some artificial ingredients than our organically-oriented core customer base.

It tasted good. And it was convenient. Those were the parameters. At a staff meeting, one of our consultants pointed out that Oregon Chai's mission was to use all natural ingredients. He was right. Technically, I wasn't "allowed" to use the tasty creamer, which was forbidden by our company's mandate, so the project was indefinitely tabled.

July of '97 was a banner month for us in terms of publicity. My first article "Oregon Chai: Tea with a Dash of Spice" was published in the Tea & Coffee Trade Journal and Heather was awarded the Business Journal's "40 Under 40" award for being one of the forty most successful and civic-minded businesspeople under the age of forty in the metro area. I was so proud.

I don't know if it was my article that brought me to the attention of Seattle's Coffee Fest but I was invited to give a seminar on chai. This would mark my first professional speaking engagement.

Carla and I left for Seattle and planned to use our new, professionally designed and built, high-tech booth. But since this was the first time the two of us had assembled it on our own following our training, I was nervous about putting it together.

We arrived at the Washington Convention Center and Carla and I unloaded the car, heaving everything - two oversized bags which held our booth, a chai dispenser, several cases of chai, paper cups, point of sale material and press kits - on top of a gigantic pushcart. Shoving and dragging our monstrosity through the parking lot, we entered the exhibit hall.

As we reached our space, we hauled the booth's various parts from their bags. It looked like a mammoth erector set. Much to our surprise, we snapped each and every little tube and bar into place and in just a few moments - voila! Our booth was up and ready for customers. We each took a few steps back, gazed at our accomplishment and grinned.

"We've sure come along way from our muslin-covered tables," Carla said.

"We sure have," I beamed in agreement.

On the second day of the exhibition, I was scheduled to give my presentation on the history of chai for the Specialty Tea Institute. I was nervous, so Carla assisted me by enduring a couple of rehearsals.

"You're probably bored out of your mind," I said after a couple of rounds.

But Carla just shook her head. "Nope. This is what our company is all about," she said. "Teamwork."

The next day I presented my speech to a group of less than twenty patrons. Despite the light turnout, they were an attentive audience, both appreciative and interested in the story of Oregon Chai. I thanked Carla for her support.

As our production levels increased, I had less and less time for trade shows. Lori now handled all the setup with Lori, Heather, Brian and our sales team manning the booth. The erector set was ably manned by our sales staff, with one rep really being the key man. He'd arrive at the show early and have our booth completely set up, with the chai mixed and in its dispensers long before the rest of us arrived. I often wondered how we found such great employees and was grateful for their loyal support. Only on rare occasions did I now attend trade shows. And when I did, I simply chatted with customers. We were a finely blended team.

A new gourmet chocolate company, Moonstruck Chocolate, opened in town. I discovered that they offered a couple of tea-flavored truffles. Chai seemed to me to be a natural progression. Shortly after my visit, I phoned them.

"You ought to make a chai truffle," I suggested.

They were familiar with Oregon Chai and already sold it in their retail outlets as a chocolate-chai beverage. They liked the idea and soon created a chai truffle in the shape of a tiny chocolate bell. They were unable to market the bells right away but a few years later I noticed that their chai bell enjoyed a majestic place of its own right in the center of their display case.

As I gazed at them, I wondered if they were the same bells we'd created years before. It was flattering knowing that Oregon Chai may have inspired this small but significant addition and that it was now surrounded by such regal company.

CHAPTER 22

Media Darlings

By September of '97, Rex Bird was not only Chairman of our Board of Directors but now also worked as part-time CEO. We hit a few major milestones this month. We sold our first entire truck load to one retail customer: Trader Joe's, and our first distributor truck load to one customer: United Grocers. With a truckload constituting 20 pallets with 75 cases per pallet, the almost $55,000 price ticket per truckload was a significant benchmark.

That same month, INC. Magazine ran an extensive article on both Heather and Oregon Chai. We seemed to have the Midas Touch when it came to publicity. Or at least Lori did. And Heather was their Golden Girl. The article included an impressive profile of Oregon Chai and stated that "Oregon Chai's packaging, point-of-purchase material, business cards and stationary are attractive and slick." I guess all that money we'd spent on marketing materials had indeed paid off. Our marketing expense amounted to less than ten percent of our sales, which was our board edict, so everything seemed to be in line with their expectations and guidance.

Another article appeared in the Statesman Journal entitled "More Tongues Tingled by Chai" and it stated: "Oregon Chai is considered a market leader and has helped create a growing national market."

Shortly after these articles were published, several television networks became interested in our story. One of the first was KPTV, a local station based in Portland.

After setting up an appointment, one of their reporters visited our office for an interview with Heather. Since he hadn't requested an interview with me, no one told me he was coming. I'd spent the entire day brewing chai before strolling into the office.

"Tedde," Brian said as I entered, sitting back in his chair, his feet atop his desk. "The reporter would also like to ask you a few questions about Oregon Chai."

I was a mess. I wasn't wearing any makeup. I had jeans on and was tired and starved from an early morning start.

"As long as I'm not on camera," I agreed.

"That's fine," the reporter said. "I usually record the interviews so I don't have to take notes - it's just for transcription purposes."

Great, I thought, as long as I'm not representing Oregon Chai looking like this. We finished the makeshift interview and I went home, eager to see what they had done with the footage of Heather.

The next day, I flicked on my TV and I was appalled to see myself, wrecked hair and spotted denim, staring out to the thousands watching this local broadcast on their TVs. But the interview was really positive. Despite my earlier reservations, my appearance wasn't nearly as bad as I'd feared and the exposure was terrific for our company.

In my search for new chai flavors, I ran across a recipe for Kashmiri chai. I remembered the car salesman telling me about his grandma's chai a couple of years earlier. After brewing it up and liking it. I was excited. Although we had earned a solid consumer base that loved the great flavor of our Original Chai recipe and were enjoying all sorts of terrific publicity for our unique new beverage, we had been warned that being limited to a solitary product was a risky business stance to maintain. Broadening our retail offerings would translate into more product fronts, which, in turn, would lead to better exposure via expanded shelf space - and ultimately, increased sales. Kashmiri chai could very well be our next product, I thought. I immediately tweaked the recipe for mass production. I also decided I wanted an herbal version of chai for our very health conscious customers.

I visited our local natural products store, sniffed the bins of aromatic herbs and spices and selected some of my favorite ingredients including mint, chamomile and lemon grass. I blended these with a bit of chamomile pollen, flower and leaves for a specific taste - and Herbal Bliss was born.

As I was creating Kashmir Green Tea and Herbal Bliss, many other companies were adding supplements to their beverages: lemon-ginger juice with Echinacea and green tea with ginseng. A few of our board members insisted that we take advantage of this trend. I disagreed.

"Our products can stand on their own," I said. "We don't need the addition of supplements."

I didn't know anything about supplements and I was afraid of adding them without knowing their possible side effects. But the board overruled me dictating that I add ginseng to the Herbal Bliss. It was chamomile-based, so to me, the stimulating ginseng defeated the purpose of the relaxing tea.

As a compromise, I suggested we add ginseng to the Kashmir Green

Tea. The board agreed. But there were two types of ginseng: Siberian ginseng also known as Eleuthro and Korean ginseng also known as red Panax.

I researched both extensively and found that if taken in large quantities over extended periods of time, Panax can have detrimental effects. It's also not recommended for pregnant women. There was no way we could control how much chai our customers consumed and I knew, because it tasted so good, they'd want lots of it. I decided caution was necessary and opted for the gentler Eleuthro. Still, I needed certainty, so I consulted a doctor of Oriental medicine who helped me determine the appropriate grams per serving of the ginseng.

The week we produced our new products developed into somewhat of a nightmare, a process I later learned was typical of the way things seemed to proceed in the food industry (not that we hadn't already had our own share of these experiences first hand).

I had been looking so forward to that week that I hadn't anticipated any problems. My anxiety about establishing a new product morphed from nervous excitement into inexplicable dread. I wondered what else could go wrong, but kept my feelings to myself in fear that I might manifest a self-fulfilling prophecy. Everything will be all right, I told myself over and over.

The ingredients were supposed to be ready a week ahead of our scheduled production, but the spice supplier hadn't included the ginseng for our new Kashmir blend. I phoned a representative immediately.

"Where's my ginseng?" I asked.

"Tedde, we thought we had plenty of ginseng in stock," he said. "But when we went to blend the product, we were out. So the Kashmir blend won't be ready in time for your scheduled pick up."

Great, I thought. I tried to stay calm and just deal with the challenges as they arose one by one, remembering what Heather always said: "Mom, business is all about solving problems. That's all we do, day in and day out."

As if by some merciless coincidence, our green tea didn't arrive either. And this event only further delayed us. But, fortunately, since our product was new, we had no tight deadline - no one was out there waiting for it - no one even knew about it yet. Luckily, our manufacturer was flexible and when all the ingredients finally arrived, squeezed us into their schedule.

From the isolated retreat of her office, Lori conducted extensive research on product-line extensions. Oregon Chai had already established a strong brand in the marketplace through its logo identity, packaging and story, so we decided we should move forward retaining the same identity. Lori urged that we maintain continuity with our logo - the oval cup icons, the word "Oregon," and the word "chai" within a black bar - on all our new products. This would help our existing customer base recognize a tried and true product with a new variation they might like to try.

To distinguish the products from one another, Lori decided to use color-coding, since color is such a key element when identifying and making a purchase. We wanted simple product-color association so that our customers could easily associate certain flavors with certain colors without disrupting our current color scheme.

Ultimately, Lori selected yellow and green for our Kashmir Green Tea, and yellow and orange for Herbal Bliss. Lori's work truly represented the marriage of her inherent artistic ability with her adept organizational skills.

One Herbal Bliss fan told me of her love for our newest addition.

"I get a lot of stomach aches," she said. "Herbal Bliss makes me feel much better. I drink it all the time."

After a promising launch, Herbal Bliss fizzled over a couple of disappointing years and was discontinued. As is often the case in the food industry (that we learned), sometimes a product will come out strong but end being nothing but a flash in the pan as just a temporary curiosity in an overly-saturated marketplace. Kashmir Green Tea, however, remained a top seller and by the end of 1997, our sales hit our projections right on the nail at $2.8 million. Our growth remained aggressive at 190%.

CNBC phoned and requested an interview with Heather. I was so excited and so proud to see her on TV. I stayed home that day, February 27, 1998, and eagerly waited through the constant promos they ran all day highlighting her story.

Finally, Bill Griffeth came on the screen and teased the segment: "Our latest 'Up and Comer' in business started a company designed to do for tea what Starbucks has done for coffee. It's called chai tea."

After their theme music intro, CNBC's Power Lunch began.

    Bill Griffeth announced: "Attention coffee drinkers. If you're tired of the same old grind, our next guest wants to win you over with a novelty tea product called chai that she hopes will be on the tables of cafes everywhere one day. Twenty-nine year old Heather Howitt runs an Oregon based beverage company, which has become a small but powerful niche player in the specialty tea market. It's even inspired Starbucks to plan its own version of chai tea. Joining us to talk about it, is our latest Up and Comer, Heather Howitt. She's in Portland, Oregon today. Good to see you. Thanks for joining us."

Heather: "Thanks, thanks for having me."

Bill: "You discovered this tea as I understand it, rather exotically in the Himalayas. Yes?"

Heather: "I was in India and noticed they were drinking this chai everywhere and started drinking it and became an addict."

Bill: "Lots of people, no doubt, did the same thing but none of them started a company to distribute it in the United States. Why did you?"

Heather: "Well, actually, after being in India, I'd gone to college at UC Santa Cruz and I noticed chai was being served in all of the cafés and espresso bars there and the same thing in Boulder, Colorado. I saw chai everywhere and thought, you know, we've got all these lattes in the Northwest, we should certainly have chai as well. And no one else was doing it, so my mother and I started a business."

Bill: "And your distribution. Where do you distribute this?"

Heather: "It's distributed nationally."

Bill: "Supermarkets?"

Heather: "Yeah, mostly natural foods markets from Fresh Fields and Bread and Circus to Whole Foods. It's also appearing now in Safeways, in the natural food sections of Fred Meyers and some of the larger chains as well as espresso bar chains like Seattle's Best Coffee and cafés."

Bill: "So it comes under the heading in that niche of the market as a natural food, is that the idea?"

Heather: "It is all natural, yes. But no, that's not necessarily the idea, that's more by chance. I would say it falls under the latte category because of the way it's prepared with milk. It's more of a tea latte."

Bill: "Speaking of which, we went out to the streets of New York, a tough crowd out there. We asked them what they thought. Gave them a taste test. Here's what they had to say."

Young businessman: "I like chai a lot. I've been drinking it for a couple months now and I just enjoy the sweetness to it, but it's not too sweet."

Smiling young woman: "It tastes like, umm..." (Thinking) "Like a cappuccino tea." She says as she smacks her lips.

Second young woman: "I thought it was very creamy and smooth and it tastes like cappuccino with ethyl."

Third woman: "I love it. It's great. It's an alternative to coffee."

Last woman: "What I like about it, you didn't have to put any sweetener in it."

Bill: "And somebody said it did taste like coffee and I tried some. We tried it with the staff this morning, with some trepidation, but you won us over as well. It is pretty good."

Heather: "Thank you."

Bill: "A full bodied tea, you achieved that.   It is almost like a coffee.   Is that the idea?"

Heather: "Well, like a latte.   After I've had too much coffee, I like to switch over to something sweet and milky. I would say it falls under the category of a hot cocoa. It's like having a vanilla latte or something like that."

Bill: "What's the business plan? Everybody's got a have a business plan, you know Heather."

Heather: "Growth!"

Bill: "You got a five year plan for this company?"

Heather: "It's growth! It's all about growth and maintaining that growth."

Bill: "How do you achieve that?"

Heather: "Well, fortunately we've had some great press. We really started in the natural food segments as well as the independent cafés and now we're starting to work with more of the chains and, um, just, just growing."

Bill: "You know we're looking at some of the numbers. The particulars of what it costs you as opposed to the sales price.   Compared to the lattes that are out there, relatively speaking, you are a little more expensive.   Can you keep that up with those kinds of profit margins without facing some tough competition out there price-wise?"

Heather: "Well actually, you can make a very similar

profit margin as you'd make with a latte. It's also less labor intensive. The product is pre-made. All you have to do is add milk and steam. You don't have to use the espresso equipment and there are some other benefits to that, as well."

Bill: "You setting up the company to be sold? Is that where you take this eventually?"

Heather: "Ah, well, we'll see. I don't want to sell it right now. That's for sure! I'm enjoying the growth, but never say never."

Bill: "Have you had any inquiries yet?"

Heather: "Ah, yes."

Bill: "And you said?"

Heather: "NO!"

Bill: "The price wasn't right, or you just aren't ready yet?"

Heather: "We didn't get that far. Yeah, we just aren't quite ready. We're just enjoying the growth."

Bill: "Well, good luck with it. We enjoyed it here and continued success to you."

Heather: "Thank you."

Bill: "Thanks for joining us today. Talking with our Up and Comer for the day, Heather Howitt, the founder of Oregon Chai, a specialty tea beverage company. She's in Portland, Oregon today."

Bill turns to the side and addresses his co-anchor: "It's pretty good. It's not bad, yeah."

At the start of the segment, the footage was odd - it looked as though Heather was staring at the floor. I asked Heather about this.

"I was watching the monitor!" she said, chuckling. "I didn't know I was on film!"

But I thought she was brilliant.

It wasn't long after this that Brian Ross resigned. I guess he felt that he had done all that he could do and that the Board had pretty much taken over his role in raising money and writing business plans. Almost all of his duties had been absorbed by other staff members, too. He left on good terms, I'm sure to go help other start-ups where the tasks were more exciting. Probably better than being stuck in perpetual board meetings and dealing with management issues.

CHAPTER 23

Will the Real Chayvalas Please Stand Up?

During my time at Oregon Chai, I frequently overheard comments from others insisting that our chai was not "real." That it wasn't "authentic." I always wondered what they meant.

"Don't worry, Mom," Heather said. "It's fine. I drank all kinds of different tasting chais in India. Ours is fine. Don't let what some people say bother you."

But I wanted to experience "chai" in its purest form myself, first hand. So, I booked a trip to the Far East.

In the waning days of March, following a long, tiring flight, my husband

and I arrived in Delhi. It was dusk and the sky shone pink. A heavy mist lingered in the warm air.

"Mmm, it smells like India," I heard another traveler say as he breathed in the ruddy haze. But I had no concept for what he meant.

The scent was unlike anything I was familiar with. It was different, a musty mix of dust and smoke that dimmed the remaining sunlight, making the whole area appear hazy. Surely this can't reflect the rest of the country, I thought. It must just be the airport.

Emerging from customs, our guide greeted us and took us to our hotel. It was large, not luxurious, but modern and comfortable. To one side of the lobby was a restaurant serving a sumptuous buffet of delectable Indian foods. As we checked in, our guide was helpful in assisting us. But then he said something very peculiar.

"May I have your passports, please?" he asked, holding out his hand.

I was shocked. I wasn't expecting this. I've never ever let go of my passport while in a foreign country. I was apprehensive about handing my passport over to someone I had just met. But he was employed through the agency that had booked our trip and he seemed trustworthy.

"I need them in order to pick up the tickets for your next flight to the state of Darjeeling in northern India," he explained. "That is where tea is grown."

Hesitantly, I handed him our passports.

On our first full day in Delhi, we met our new guide, an Indian man in his early forties. He was plump, like someone who lives comfortably but doesn't get much exercise. He was dressed in slacks and a short-sleeved, white cotton shirt. We chatted for a while and embarked on a car tour of the city.

"I'm mainly interested in seeing where chai is sold," I said.

Leaning on the back of the front seat, he turned around and grinned, waving one chubby hand in the misty air.

"Sure, sure," he said. "There are lots of wonderful places to see." Our driver gunned the engine and we were off.

Amid congested streets, buffalos pulling wagons and cows wandering everywhere, he showed us Gandhi's tomb, several Muslim temples and lavish Hindu shrines. As we traveled, the driver blasted his horn wherever we went. Finally, with no help from our guide who was taking us to all the popular tourist locations, I finally found what I was searching for: at the security gate leading to one historical spot, with no sign marking it, I saw a young man selling chai.

On his small cart stood a propane burner. I watched with fascination as he tossed tea and cardamom pods into a pan of boiling milk. After it had brewed to his satisfaction, he poured the hot liquid through a sieve and into a small glass cup, then added lots of sugar.

Preceding our trip, I had purchased filtered straws to drink with, having no desire to spend my time in India being ill. Hoping I wouldn't offend the friendly fellow by using it, I grabbed one from my pocket, lifted the cup to my lips and sipped. It was good. Not like Oregon Chai, but very sweet, milky - with just a hint of spice. He smiled and nodded, not seeming to mind that I'd used a straw.

As we toured Delhi, I marveled at its contrasts. Everywhere I looked, I saw poverty. Yet nearly every Indian woman, whether a professional or living on the streets, wore striking saris tinted in brilliant shades of red, green, blue and gold. I learned they consisted of five heavy yards of fabric and whether sweeping out their one-room houses or washing dishes in water seeping from pipes into the street, the women wore their saris in the ninety-plus degree heat.

I saw scores of adorable children with large, brown eyes. At the stoplights, some would scamper to our car begging for change. I was frightened that the heavy, congested traffic would run them over. At one of the famous monuments, I gave them some of the children sugarless candy.

"Don't do that!" our guide yelled. "If they get rewarded for begging, they won't go to school."

"But it's just a few pieces of candy," I said.

"Yes, but all the guides in India ask the visitors to please not give to the beggars," he said.

All I wanted to do was help.

That evening, just as our guide had promised, our passports were returned. Relieved, my husband and I decided we'd take an after-dinner stroll through Delhi. It was like another world. Cars and trucks honked their horns incessantly. Drivers honk instead of signaling to one another their intent to turn or pass. Each passing truck had a sign, "blow horn," printed on its rear. All whizzed past us at lightning speeds.

As we walked, we noticed the housing across the street. Just a few blocks from our modern hotel stood hundreds of shacks constructed of cardboard or whatever leftover building materials their homeless occupants could find.

As we gazed at the shelters, strolling down the sidewalk of a major thoroughfare, I saw a little girl all alone. She looked like she couldn't be more than two years old. She was just wandering along the edge of the road. I gasped, holding my breath as she stepped from the curb and into the street where giant trucks roared past. Then she did something I've never witnessed in my entire life (and hope I never do again): she squatted in the gutter and peed. When she finished, she clambered back up onto the curb and toddled back down the street.

"David!" I shouted. "Did you see that? I can't believe she wasn't injured!" I was frightened for her life.

We turned, walked a bit further and noticed a young boy who looked about twelve or thirteen, sitting in the road next to the sidewalk. His legs were a bent, tangled mess and he wore only a wrinkled navy blazer encrusted with dirt. It looked as though he'd slept in it. I turned and looked at my husband.

"I've read that some beggars are intentionally crippled so tourists will be more sympathetic and give them more money," I said, wondering if that could possibly be the case with this poor little boy.

After about an hour, we wandered back to our hotel, the little boy still on my mind.

That night I awoke at 3:00 a.m. I wanted to rush down to that grungy corner, take that boy into my arms and carry him home with me. When David finally awoke, I told him about my concern.

"We have to go back," I said.

"Tedde, you can't take all of India with you," he whispered.

The next day, we went back to the same corner, I had no idea what I could do, but I wanted to do something. But the little boy was gone.

The next afternoon, while wandering through Delhi on our own, my husband and I discovered another fellow selling chai in a street market. He created his in the same fashion as the first, by boiling milk in a pan on a small hot plate. Like the one we'd found earlier, his chai was also brewed with the simplest of ingredients.

The next morning, in our hotel's restaurant, I requested chai.

"You want masala chai? Indian chai?" the waiter asked.

"Yes," I said.

He smiled, looking pleased and trotted off to retrieve it. After a few minutes he returned, handing me a teapot filled with hot water and a bowl of finely ground spices resembling instant cocoa. I didn't recognize it.

"What is this?" I asked.

"Chai," he answered.

I peered at the bowl.

"Where does it come from?" I asked, looking up at the waiter.

"Would you like to see the box?" he asked.

"Yes," I said. It sounded intriguing.

A few moments later, he returned with a small carton containing a powdered, instant chai mix. Oh no! Am I too late to find "real" chai even in India? Here I was on my quest to taste authentic chai and they'd worked out the powdered version? Even in the birthplace of chai, processing and commercialization had infiltrated the market.

Later that day, our guide drove us toward Agra, the site of the Taj Mahal. Along the way, we stopped at a restaurant and again I ordered chai, wondering what I'd get. Soon, the waiter brought me a small, stainless steel pitcher filled with chai, much more like the chai I knew. I sipped it and smiled. It was delicious, far better than most of the chais I'd sampled. To my delight, it tasted very much like our Oregon Chai.

"How do you prepare this?" I asked our server.

He spoke only broken English, but understood. He nodded, turned, strode back into the kitchen and returned with a saucer filled with a variety of whole spices. I recognized many of them. I was pleased and relieved.

"Mission accomplished," I said to my husband. "Oregon Chai is authenticated!"

On our return from Agra, we passed vast golden fields of sweet sugar cane. Near one meadow, I noticed a woman in a vivid gold sari walking by the side of the road hefting a one-foot-high load of eight-foot-long cane stalks atop her head. Even with the immense weight, the woman strode with apparent ease. We saw buffalo and camels hauling trailers filled with cane stalks. At one field, I asked our driver to stop.

"I want to take some pictures of the harvest," I said.

As I stood clicking off pictures a few field workers approached and spoke with us. They were all smiles, nodding and saying only "Hello."

One offered me a small piece of sugar cane to take back home. I gladly accepted.

From Delhi, we boarded a plane east where we met our next tour guide. After a two and a half hour drive ascending a narrow, steep and snaking road through the foothills of the Himalayas, we reached Darjeeling, purported to grow the best tea in the world. The weather was cold and damp. When we finally arrived, I felt horrible.

"My neck hurts so bad, I just want to cry," I told my husband.

"It's probably from carrying those two liters of bottled water in your backpack," he said.

He was right. It may have been silly for me to have lugged them along, but becoming ill from drinking tainted tap water was not in my tour plans.

"Well, it's better to be safe and bring my own than take a chance on not finding any bottled water in this remote area," I said.

I rubbed my aching shoulders, grabbed my burdensome backpack and tread on toward our night's lodging.

At our hotel in Darjeeling, the first thing I did was inquire about a massage. Less than an hour after our arrival, a masseur arrived in our room, providing the best massage I'd ever had. When he finished, I felt rejuvenated. For only seven U.S. dollars, I had received an hour of bliss. I awarded him a large tip.

Our hotel room was spacious with soaring ceilings and lots of view windows. The recently remodeled bathroom had a brand new pedestal sink. But there was one problem: there was water all over the floor. We searched and searched but couldn't figure out the source of the leak. After a few hours of investigation, my husband finally deduced that the drainpipe from the new sink went down onto the floor and simply ended. It drained directly onto the floor, which was sloped slightly so that the water ran from the bottom of the sink across the floor and into a hole in the wall and then outside. Not the plumbing to which I'd become accustomed, but certainly a new experience.

With no central heating, the hotel and consequently our room, were both chilly. But our room did have a fireplace. I strolled to the lobby and spoke with the attendant.

"Do you have any wood for our fireplace?" I asked.

"Yes, yes, I'll bring you some," he said.

After a few minutes he arrived to our room and as I opened the door, I could hardly contain my amusement. Our "wood" consisted of a half-gallon-sized cardboard container filled with kindling.

"Here is your wood," he said, smiling.

"Oh," I said. "That's all? Umm, thank you."

"Yes, my pleasure," he said, still grinning.

I handed him a tip, closed the door and turned toward David as I held the box of kindling.

"Well, here's our wood for the night," I said.

He chuckled. "Well, it's a good thing we have this electric heater, too," he said, pointing toward the corner of the room.

The heater bore only three legs so that it leaned to one side and wobbled. But it worked. I sat in front of it for two hours.

Electricity in Darjeeling was available only four hours a day, from seven to nine in the morning and again from seven to nine at night. This schedule included all of the shops in the center of town. I arrived unprepared for the cold weather, so I went hunting for a coat or a sweater the first thing the next morning.

The shopping district resided on a steep, slender road that wound through the heart of town. The shops were small, about the size of a single-car garage and open completely to the street.

At one, I found a vendor selling gorgeous wool shawls from Kashmir. In another, several female Tibetan refugees were sitting on the concrete floor knitting. Hanging on one of their racks, I discovered a stunning wool cardigan with hand-hewn wooden buttons for just twenty-five U.S. dollars. I snatched it up and handed the clerk my money. One of the women smiled at me.

"I knitted that sweater myself," she said.

I smiled back. "It's absolutely beautiful," I said. "I can't wait to put it on."

After I returned from my cold-weather clothing jaunt, we visited the tea gardens. Here I discovered women performing all of the harvesting. The native tea plant, camellia sinensis, is a member of the camellia family, knowledge I'd learned from my years in the tea industry. In the wild, these plants can grow very tall but on the tea estates, workers prune them to about waist level, making picking the delicate buds and leaves easier for the women. I watched as they harvested the plants.

"Women are better suited for the work than men," one worker said as I stood gazing about, "because of their small hands."

I wondered if this was really true. Nevertheless, the women here also wore the same brightly colored saris, transforming them into brilliant flowers against the infinite fields of green.

Each woman toted a large bag on her back and after it was filled, would hike up a steep hill, descend down a dirt road and into a processing plant where the tea was laid out in fifty to one-hundred-foot-long trays.

The green tea was quickly dried and packaged while the black tea was dried longer to oxidize it in order to obtain the expected flavor and color after brewing. It was fascinating to see the tea laid out in giant bins.

From Darjeeling, we traveled to Calcutta, where we met our new guide who we learned was a professor of linguistics at a local university. After some chitchat, he asked where we'd like to go.

"I need to learn as much as possible about tea," I said. "And chai in particular."

"Certainly," he said. "There are many places I can show you."

He was friendly, warm-hearted and eager to help.

Along the way, on the lively streets of Calcutta, I noticed large, black iron instruments each including a giant, circular, geared crank.

"What are those?" I asked, pointing at the gears.

"Oh, yes," our guide said. "Those are wringers. They're used to crush sugar canes. By turning the crank, clamps squeeze the sweet juice from the stalk. Vendors sell the juice by the glass and many people drink it daily as a treatment for hepatitis."

"Oh," I said, nodding my head. I remembered reading on the web that drinking cane juice on the streets may be the primary source of Hepatitis A - but I kept that information to myself. Luckily, we hadn't tried any.

Our first stop was the Tea Board of India, where I learned more about the extensive history of chai.

"Masala chai was invented by Ayurvedic doctors who tended the Indian raja and his court," the curator said. "The Ayuvedic practice is an ancient system of natural medicine."

"The ingredients in chai were chosen for their beneficial properties. Ginger and cardamom are good for digestion, especially after a supper of hot Indian curry. In the morning, the tea in chai helps you wake up, milk provides nourishment and you get a rush of energy from all the sugar."

"Please, tell me more," I said. I wanted to soak in everything I possibly could.

"There is no actual recipe for the quintessential chai," the curator went on. "Some Indians report that their grandmother made it for them as children using whatever spices were available. Recipes were often family secrets. Depending upon the availability of spices or old family recipes, the flavors can vary quite a bit."

The curator then led us into the room where tea auctions were held.

"Some of the brokers' families have had a seat at the auction for generations," he said.

Before we departed, The Tea Board referred me to a local tea grower and exporter then our guide returned us to our hotel.

Later that afternoon, the exporter's driver picked me up at our hotel and drove me through the willowy streets of Calcutta to an old, wooden building.

"This is the Chowringhee Mansion," he said.

Even though I couldn't pronounce most of them, I loved the mesmerizing sounds of the Indian names.

We entered through a small, timber door at the side of the front of the building and I held my breath as we rode the primitive wooden elevator to the upper floors of the ancient structure. Arriving at our floor, he heaved open the elevator's metal gate and we stepped out into the reception area.

The exporter's office occupied several floors, with narrow hallways and low ceilings. We ambled past small rooms where men in white shirts worked among endless piles of paper stacked everywhere. Soon, we reached the tea-tasting room, where we found about two hundred various types ready for sampling. For each tea, a tiny mound of fresh tea leaves, a cup of the brewed tea, one spoon and one small saucer of the used tealeaves sat ready for their taster.

"To begin, the taster first smells and feels the tea leaves," the exporter said. "Then the taster slurps the liquor from the spoon, making a loud noise and sloshes it around in the mouth. Satisfied with the taste, the taster will then spit the tea into a large spittoon."

"Great," I said, seeing the similarity to wine tasting, "I'll give it a try."

But I was too inhibited to spit. Instead, I sampled spoonfuls of a few of the teas that the exporter recommended for use in chai and then swallowed. But he noticed my trepidation.

"It would be impossible for a professional tea-taster to sample over two hundred teas a day without spitting them out," he said, grinning at my obvious reticence.

When I returned to our room, I was exhausted. Like Delhi, the heat in Calcutta was oppressive. But despite my fatigue, I felt I had accomplished what I'd set out to do: sample and learn everything I could about "authentic" Indian chai. I had worked enough. Now I could relax and enjoy the rest of my vacation.

In Calcutta, we lodged at the reasonably priced, five-star Taj Bengal hotel. It was several stories high with a large, central atrium and an Olympic-sized swimming pool in its garden of palm trees and fragrant, tropical flowers. Upscale boutiques and four gourmet restaurants resided off the main lobby. It offered everything I needed without even venturing out into the heat. Now this was a vacation and I planned to luxuriate in every minute of it. I realized that my hard work at Oregon Chai was beginning to pay off and I liked the feeling. All of the work and sacrifices might have been worth the effort after all and it felt good!

Our hotel was located just three blocks from the local zoo, the same zoo we had strolled through just a few days earlier, where we'd seen a tree packed with large, foot-long bats. During our final night in India, from the comfort of our room, we saw the same bats fly weightlessly past our window, like birds migrating in the spring, quiet and peaceful, soaring past the fading sun through the hazy, pink Indian sky.

The next morning, we departed India via Singapore, where we spent six hours dozing in the airport hotel. We enjoyed a quick stopover in Hong Kong and after fifteen more hours on the plane, arrived bleary-eyed in Los Angeles. At customs an inspector asked if I had anything to declare.

"Nothing," I said.

"Do you have any agriculture products?" he said.

I thought about his question and suddenly remembered the gift I'd been given.

"Well," I said. "I do have a little piece of sugar cane."

"Let me see it," he demanded.

It took several minutes of rummaging through my luggage before I found the little bag where the sugar cane was safely stored. I handed it to him. He laughed and held it up high so that everyone going through customs could see it.

"Hey, look, can you believe it?" he shouted. "This lady is trying to smuggle cane sugar through customs."

The other inspectors laughed. I felt everyone's eyes on me. I was tired, confused and very embarrassed.

"I just wanted to show it to my partners," I said finally.

"Well, I'm sorry," he said. "But you can't bring it into the country - that's the rule."

I didn't understand why and was too tired to ask. So the tiny stalk, the same one I'd so carefully packaged and carried all throughout India, got tossed in the Los Angeles Airport Customs' trash.

If You Like That, Try This!

One morning, we received a call from one of the largest coffee distributors in the country, expressing interest in Oregon Chai. But they wanted a private label. We had already decided against manufacturing under any label other than our own. Our primary goal was branding our product and a private label would dilute our efforts.

But both the board and the sales team wanted the distributor's business. Against my opposing vote, the board decided we'd go forward and pack our Oregon Chai concentrate using their label and their name.

The container they wanted was unavailable through our co-packer, so the chai was brewed and then loaded into tankers and shipped to another facility where it was successfully packaged for the distributor. In the end, they were pleased with the product results but their customers were certain it was not the original product. Many claimed it didn't even taste the same. After a few months, the company decided that the Oregon Chai brand itself offered a better sale and the entire private-labeling project was dropped. The experience ultimately proved the power of branding.

A broader audience and more market appeal was another one of our goals. We decided kosher certification of all of our products was a practical idea. I am not Jewish so this was yet another new area for me but I found it fascinating and enjoyed researching everything kosher. I learned that the Jewish people have great respect for the animals they eat and are especially considerate that they not consume milk and beef at the same meal. They do not want to drink the milk from a mother cow while eating her calf. Fortunately tea, and consequently our chai concentrate, is kosher. So we sought its certification.

Over the first couple of years, Heather continued visiting Starbucks, each time hoping they'd snatch up our product for their burgeoning business. But the last couple of meetings ended only in frustration.

On her last trip, Heather asked that our sales consultant join her in Seattle, requiring that he fly in from San Francisco. After arriving at the Starbucks' Seattle office, the pair were kept waiting for three hours, only to learn that Starbucks had decided they'd produce chai without our help.

Some staff members expressed concern that this could harm us significantly. But I was convinced otherwise. With Starbucks mega advertising dollars raising the awareness of chai throughout the entire country. I was certain it could only help us.

When Starbucks launched their own chai tea latte they ran full-page ads in the local paper. We looked at the ad and saw a thinly veiled version of our great (and expensive) slogan. Their campaign was: "Think of it as Nirvana. In a cup" in close comparison to our: "Nirvana, now available by the cup." It's ironic to note that we had paid just about as much for this slogan as they had offered us initially for our recipe.

Heather initiated swift action to prevent marketplace confusion. Not intimidated by this industry giant, we requested that Starbucks cease using their slogan that was so incredibly close to ours. We clarified: so incredibly close to our trademarked slogan. After a little nudging from our attorney, they graciously complied. If further legal steps had been necessary, it would've been a pretty obvious case but likely prohibitively expensive for us - so we were glad to resolve it quickly and quietly. As I had hoped, their ad campaign helped to drive our sales even higher.

Sometimes developing and demonstrating new products to the staff was a terrific challenge. Our board decided they would like me to work on a concentrate with less sugar. I wanted a sugar-free chai but couldn't summon sufficient support from our staff.

I tried convincing them by offering samples. I prepared the concentrate and set it down in the center of the room as we were conducting a staff meeting. Then I left momentarily, searching for sweetener. But before I could return, they'd tasted the unsweetened chai and gulped up all the samples. I returned to sour faces and the sounds of "ugh" floating throughout the room.

"You haven't even given me a chance," I said. "An unsweetened product gives all of our customers a choice. They can add as much or as little sugar as they like, or even use a sugar substitute."

I lobbied adamantly for an unsweetened rather than a less-sweetened chai. But in the end, I was overruled, seemingly as always. I didn't agree with our team's decision, but proceeded with the development of the less-sweet concentrate, just as they requested.

Heather was now Oregon Chai's CEO and I was the Vice President of Production but no longer on the Board. I met with Heather to seek assistance in determining the sweetness level for our new, Not-So-Sweet concentrate. Every formula we'd developed until now had required enormous work and energy. In our office, we'd tested a chai without sugar that was vetoed, one with nine grams of sugar and one with thirteen. Everyone liked the thirteen-gram formula best. Sure, I surmised, of course they like the thirteen grams best: it's the sweetest.

I'd researched sales for unsweetened products and they were dismal. I also discovered that other products with just nine grams of sugar sold better than those with thirteen. Regardless, our team wanted the thirteen-gram formula. I tried holding out, believing that professional help would settle the dispute. I called the head of the sensory division in the Food Science Department at Oregon State University and then told Heather of my proposed study with OSU. Her response was negative.

"We don't need to do a market study," she insisted.

"But the cost will be absorbed easily by the startup costs of the product," I explained. "I've included sensory tests in the total start-up costs. We could cover everything by selling a mere thirty-two hundred cases. That should be simple enough."

But Heather had other impending financial worries. She was not feeling generous.

"I want to do it," I said with finality.

"Well, okay," she said, "if you think it's that important."

I e-mailed my contact at OSU immediately asking that she begin the process. Unfortunately, just as Heather had foreseen, the sensory tests were inconclusive. Both the nine grams and the thirteen grams emerged nearly equal. We produced our concentrate with thirteen grams of sugar.

A few years later, Oregon Chai reformulated the less-sweet chai and produced one with only 5 grams of sugar, Oregon Chai Slightly Sweet concentrate.

In December of 1998, Fresh Cup reported that chai had moved to the mainstream and that Oregon Chai remained the leader in the category.

In March of 1999, Oregon Chai was securely the top-selling brand of chai with an over 65.7% market share - among almost 100 competitors that had popped up in the category we had created. Lori put together new promotional materials. We needed the best sales statistics we could find to beef up the credibility of our marketing approach. We turned to the SPINS report, a subscription service that tracks the purchasing habits of consumers, most relevant to us, from sales figures from natural food stores.

Our Original concentrate was the number-one selling flavor in both the tea and chai categories. Kashmir Green Tea was the number-two selling chai flavor as well as the number-three selling flavor in the entire tea category. Herbal Bliss rounded out the third spot, as well as coming in eighth in the tea category. According to SPINS, the chai category had grown nearly eighty percent with Oregon Chai's growth reported at one hundred eighty percent. We were ecstatic.

In June of that same year, a group of seniors from the School of Business at the University of Oregon conducted a marketing project for us surveying customers. We were surprised to learn that chai awareness was higher than they'd expected. We'd been selling chiefly in the natural food-store segment and the group recommended we move into mass market, suggesting we try attaining eye-level product display.

"There are so many products on the shelves and so many distractions," they urged, "that you need to grab your customer's attention. Make it easy for them to find your product."

According to their study, the majority of chai consumers ranged in age from twenty-three to forty and reported that the main reason they selected Oregon Chai was because they liked the taste, confirming for us that product tasting was the surest way to promote our chai.

After a great deal of research on both chai and tea sales, the specific demographics of our customers and all the latest industry trends, we handed it all over to yet another ad agency who used this information to further promote our Oregon Chai story.

After several years of remarkable growth, I came to the realization that I needed help. But I was afraid that if I hired an experienced professional, I might be putting myself out of a job.

I was terrified. I loved Oregon Chai but was exhausted from the long, grueling hours it demanded. Each batch now consisted of 20,000 - 60,000 gallons of concentrate and cost more than the appraised value of my home. The result was my stomach knotting every time we manufactured. It was such a major undertaking. I knew nothing about the processor's immense, complex equipment. If something went awry, I was concerned I would either not catch it or not know what to do if I did. I was so tired and so stressed, that it seemed I was continuously on the verge of tears. My emotional state could also have been the result of menopause rearing its hot-flashing, emotional head, too. Hiring an assistant appeared my only option.

After one particularly draining afternoon of brewing, I finally plunked my weary self down and composed two job descriptions: one for me and one for my potential assistant. I retained the tasks I enjoyed most: cost analysis, planning, scheduling and purchasing and delegated on-site supervision and the development of quality control procedures to my new assistant.

Though I'd created a few methods of my own, I felt we needed more, insuring that our chai remained consistently the "best in the world." Also, since I was always a cautious cook and not terribly creative - I could never afford throwing away a meal I'd botched, I always followed recipes carefully; I wanted someone who could oversee new product development. I wanted that off my plate. The new products I had developed were the result of research and lots of experiments but had little resemblance to real science or creativity. I didn't develop new products out of passion, I'd developed our line extensions out of necessity. It really wasn't my calling.

Oregon Chai now enjoyed the financial power to hire consultants, trained food scientists who relished this type of work. I had to admit to myself and finally to others, I really had no interest in doing that any more.

I showed my two job descriptions to Heather and our Chairman of the Board, who both approved them immediately. After several interviews, we finally found someone with several years experience in the beverage industry and offered him the position. He had worked in large processing facilities, had a good sense of humor and was enthusiastic about Oregon Chai. He seemed the ideal candidate. I was excited to have some help and looked forward to a long relationship.

CHAPTER 25

Wait, This Isn't What I Asked For!

When he first started, my new assistant and I worked well together. He got along great with the rest of the staff. But after a few weeks, problems arose.

At about the same time that my assistant came aboard, Kurt, now our Vice President of Finance purchased new accounting software. It had cost analysis and inventory control programs, which required course instruction. I attended the class on inventory control. After I'd completed the class, I discovered that my assistant had attended the classes for costing, raw materials inventory and finished goods inventory. But I had wanted to attend the class for costing and I complained to Kurt.

"Don't worry," he said. "You'll go in the future. Your assistant is already familiar with the software so it was easier to train him and get him up and running first."

I felt betrayed but acquiesced and continued tracking our materials, scheduling and finished goods with Microsoft Excel. Then, one morning, I heard a rap on my office door.

"Come in," I called.

It was Heather. She had just come from a meeting with the Board Chair.

"I want you involved in new product development," she said.

"But, Heather, I don't want to do that any more."

I thought that would be the end of it.

Initially, my assistant and I attended the meetings with product innovators together. But after just a few months, he became unavailable for them, insisting he was needed at the processing plant. I understood. We were very busy and he was needed there. So I began attending the meetings alone - still doing what I thought I had hired an assistant to take over for me. Well, this'll shake itself out, I thought. Foolishly.

I told my assistant about the eleven-ounce container I had seen at the National Food Processors' Association. He agreed that the box would be a great solution for our ready-to-drink product. Our co-packer had just purchased the machines necessary to pack eleven-ounce containers and was seeking uses for them. This was our opportunity.

While at the plant, we tested both the Original chai and the Kashmir Green Tea, blending some freshly made concentrate of each with soy milk. When we tasted it, it was delicious. And the most promising aspect of this experiment was that unlike cow's milk, soy milk tolerated heat. The soy-chai combination was tasty - and the soy didn't burn. More importantly, the cost, compared with that of glass, was much more reasonable.

Our sales consultant was excited about the new soy-chai product and shipped one of our customers a couple of sample cases. They tried it and liked it so much that they wanted a truckload. We were astonished. Although I was pleased, I hadn't yet received the go-ahead from our management or Board.

As the days passed, I became more and more frustrated as I waited for project approval. Then, one day, I received an e-mail asserting the board was "getting pretty impatient" about the new chai-soy beverage. I sent a return email asking what they meant. I learned to my frustration that the board members were under the impression that we were going ahead with production - but no one had bothered to tell me we were greenlit to move forward. I had been sitting around, bored and dismayed, waiting for their approval. I spoke with Lori who, by this time, was our Vice President of Marketing.

"Did you know the board wanted us to move forward with the new soy ready-to-drink?" I asked.

Her eyes widened and she shook her head.

"No, I had no idea they were ready to move forward with the project," she said. "And I have no package designed."

"Well, I guess we have to get moving," I said. "I wish someone would have said something. I've been so excited about it. I would have jumped at the chance to start this project."

At once, the new product emerged as our highest priority. The board wanted it and they wanted it NOW! Production was geared up and ready to go but we had no packaging so we couldn't move forward - we had nothing to put it in. Since the company making our packaging was based in Switzerland, printing in their new German plant was required for the quickest turnaround. But in order that we'd have sufficient packaging for the first run, some would require air freighting stateside.

So, functioning as print supervisor, Lori flew to Germany and just a few days later, our new packaging was delivered. We titled our newest, ready-to-drink beverages Soy Tea Lattes. I was satisfied with our new product and greatly relieved that the project we had worked on for so long was finally accomplished.

In July of 1999, following numerous studies on soy, the F.D.A. stated that beverage companies could include on their labels a claim that soy proteins may reduce the risk of developing heart disease - but our legal counsel cautioned us against making such claims. Seeking a second opinion, I questioned one of our manufacturing plant food scientists.

"Two servings of your soy beverage a day have enough soy protein to satisfy the claim," he said. "But just one serving does not."

I was satisfied with his answer and felt it best that we leave the information off the packaging, as our attorney recommended. There wasn't much room on the containers for more copy anyway and I hoped our customers would discover the benefits of soy on their own and consequently seek out our product.

Heather and the board still hoped for a ready-to-drink with milk packaged in a small, glass bottle. We contracted a company to develop a ready-to-drink dairy beverage. They started with eight flavors - which were soon reduced to four: Original, Chocolate, Peach and Kashmir. The chocolate, which I wanted marketed as an adult drink, was heavily fortified with guarana, ginseng and gingko biloba as a stimulant providing the consumer with additional energy.

The peach was also tasty, though I was concerned its appeal was limited since not everyone enjoys peach-flavored items. It also included hibiscus, then a widely unknown herb. We positioned the peach as a feel-good drink, reasoning it would appeal to women because of its aroma and fuzzy, peach-like texture. We also decided adding a bit of chamomile and kava root would provide additional market appeal, branding this chai as a relaxing, bedtime beverage.

The original chai presented the real challenge. The food scientist now working on the project told us from the outset that achieving the same flavor in a glass-packed chai as that of a fresh product was nearly impossible. But they tried anyway. Still, no matter what they attempted, they couldn't eradicate that burnt-milk taste.

We carted our new flavored ready-to-drink beverages over to a professional marketing firm for sensory testing. The chocolate scored high enough that the agency recommended we market it. The original ready-to-drink chai still had a strong scalded taste and needed further refinement. After the marketing test, we decided that we simply could not go forward with the project since the cost for launching the new line would run at least a quarter of a million dollars - and we wouldn't even have our flagship original as one of the products.

Heather also desired a super-charged chai. We decided against adding coffee since baristas could easily add a shot of espresso to a chai latte should customers want more caffeine. Their counter space is severely limited anyhow, I thought, so why would they buy another flavor?

Herbs were popular. The chocolate ready-to-drink we'd already developed included stimulating herbs, so I ran my idea past Lori and Heather.

"We could add the herbs to the original to give it a zing," I said.

"I like it!" Lori said.

"Yes," said Heather, "and we can call it Chai Charger."

Several of our board members suggested we try a chai-flavored ice cream since ice cream drizzled with or made from scratch at home with Oregon Chai concentrate was delicious. One of our sales managers studied its potential. After extensive research, he believed chai ice cream could sell well, based upon the success of the chai category.

At this time, Ben and Jerry's Ice Cream offered a chai sorbet that sold well. However, breaking into the increasingly limited space in the frozen food sections of the retail outlets was generally difficult for a small company. It was commonly monopolized by large companies that could afford to manage the space their products occupy by visiting the stores daily. We couldn't afford this kind of manpower attention. It's no surprise that small companies find controlling their shelf space much more difficult.

Our sales manager recommended we attempt co-branding with a bigger company, offering a chai ice cream under both brands. Ultimately, he just couldn't recommend launching an ice cream, believing we were simply too small and might risk losing our focus. He'd worked for a large company previously that had tried launching multiple items all within one year and had failed with every one. He insisted that it would significantly stretch our already-limited resources - and that we should stay focused in the beverage category.

A primary goal for me remained in product development, maximizing chai applications. While this wasn't my preference and I never felt quite qualified to perform this function beyond trial and error and good old common sense, there wasn't anybody else yet to do it, so I hung in there.

I loved chocolate and thought, mixed with chai, it might make a tasty drink. I experimented with several variations of cocoa and discovered chocolate was much more of a challenge than I'd anticipated. It was also a hard sell.

When questioned, people believed chai and chocolate didn't go together. But I thought it was still a good idea worth pursuing, so I worked on it until I finally crafted one I liked. Then I offered everyone at Oregon Chai a sample. Their response was less than enthusiastic.

"The majority of our business is food service," Heather explained. "A barista can easily add a bit of chocolate syrup to an Original Chai latte. So why would they need to buy a chocolate flavored chai?"

Everyone agreed and the project was tabled.

Despite a lack of interest, one of our sales managers believed a chocolate flavor would do well in retail, so once again I plucked the cocoa from my cupboard. In my initial trials, I had worked with Ghirardelli chocolate, but when I phoned them inquiring about availability, I learned they were experiencing problems at their cocoa processing facility, resulting in six-week processing delays.

I next contacted ADM who offered a delicious Dutch cocoa. They shipped samples and referred me to someone in their research and development department where I was offered more information on formulating our product. I continued to work with the Ghirardelli cocoas as I thought customers would recognize the Ghirardelli brand.

I produced four variations: two with Ghirardelli and two with ADM and offered our staff samples of each. One Ghirardelli and one ADM were comparable. I then presented our staff with samples of regular chocolate milk for comparison with our new chocolate chai. The chai infused the chocolate with a punch resulting in a delectable, chocolate adult drink.

"This is pretty good," one member said.

"Yes, I like it," said another.

Kurt, our VP of Finance gulped six cups.

"This will be Oregon Chai's newest sensation," I said.

Initially, the Board was concerned about using Ghirardelli chocolate, not wanting us coupled with only one supplier.

I asked Lori her opinion.

"Well," she said, "I think the Ghirardelli connection will be positive."

I nodded.

Heather's opinion made it unanimous.

We conducted a test run of both the chocolate concentrate and a chocolate ready-to-drink with soy. Both turned out delicious but we opted for the chocolate concentrate rather than the chocolate-soy beverage since the concentrates were more versatile. Consumers could add them to either milk or soy so that those who did not like or were allergic to soy could enjoy them, too. Our profit margins were also better with the concentrates. From a business standpoint, it was a no brainier. My assistant added a bit of Xantham gum that gave our new product slightly more texture. I liked the results.

Our product development and diversification was going gang-busters. Heather's Oregon Chai Charger was a finalist for Outstanding New Product at the 1999 NASFT's summer Fancy Food Show in New York.

Another part of my job, one which I enjoyed most, was sourcing raw ingredients. They had to be one-hundred percent natural and quality

was the number one attribute. I also tried to buy organic ingredients whenever I could find them. Organic spices were sometimes a challenge and our honey supplier laughed when I asked him about organic honey. He said, "How can you track the bees? How do you know if they wonder off and get into a field of non-organic clover or flowers?" Good questions but I continued my search.

I was proud to say we did find a company that shared many of our values, ForesTrade. They helped indigenous people cultivate organic spices in the rain forest regions of the world thereby preventing the cutting and damaging of some of earth's most valuable resources. Oregon Chai became one of ForestTrade's largest customers.

In spite of the many successes, I began to sense that my value at Oregon Chai was waning. I was exhausted from working sixty plus hours a week but our company was not publicly owned and there was no golden parachute for me should I decide to leave.

I had no contract, no requirement for severance pay and therefore couldn't support myself and would have to attain other employment after all this time. Isn't that where I started all this? Looking for a job?

The other founders were exhausted, too and hoping for more of a reward for all of our hard work and struggles. We needed a solution. We found a company interested in investing. They were willing to buy part of our shares. I was relieved. Selling a few shares would provide me much-needed income, affording me the opportunity to begin planning my exit from the company.

Everyone on our team was excited about the possibility, since everything we owned was tied up in Oregon Chai and this would allow us to cash out, to actually finally profit from all of our hard work and faith.

We struck a deal with the company and they requested the necessary documents. Before signing a contract with us, the investors required extensive information about our company, kind of like a loan package, known in the business as "due diligence." The paperwork took the better part of a year to complete and included:

* a history of our business, including any previous companies
* an organizational chart
* a copy of the office lease
* our accounting policies
* a complete list of shareholders
* the names of our co-packers, any potential new co-packers and copies of their contracts
* billing policies
* lists of customers and food brokers and how long we had worked with them
* projected sales volumes
* details on distribution arrangements
* copies of the mass market study prepared by one of our consultants
* the impact of mass market pricing on our margins
* estimated amount of capital needed to penetrate the mass market channel
* lists of major food service distributors and the arrangements we had with each
* an estimate of the size and growth of both the food service and retail market
* current market penetration
* details on scheduled customer promotions
* any customers who refused to take the product and why
* the company's current branding strategy
* how our products were positioned against the competitors in the market
* planned changes in the branding strategy
* our brand extensions and new product strategies
* three references for each of the major executives

* copies of any benefit policies
* breakdown of salaries and equity ownership for senior management
* a list of senior executives who had left the company along with their reasons for leaving
* whether or not we expected any new hires over the next year and their position and salary
* copies of all organizational documents; charter and bylaws
* copies of minutes of board meetings and copies of all trademark filings
* audited, historical financials all monthly cash flow and balance sheets
* a detailed breakdown of marketing expenses
* a detailed breakdown of revenue and costs by product
* accounts receivable and accounts payable
* an analysis of bad debt and other reserves
* our general terms of all loans and notes payable
* copies of our income tax returns
* an explanation of any extraordinary and non-recurring expenses
* detailed cash flow projections by month
* revenue forecasts by product and by outlet
* and finally a list of all major competitors as well as the historical performance of these competitors, including revenues and market share.

Our able staff eventually pulled together all of the information that the investment bankers requested and Oregon Chai soon acquired an ever-growing staff of competent advisors who became actively involved with our board. It was now time for these newest members to begin penning the next chapters of the Oregon Chai story. And it was now time for me to start thinking about what I wanted to do with my own future.

Tedde and Carla at CoffeeFest in Seattle, 1996

Tedde testing cane syrup, 1996

Nirvana in a Cup: The founding of Oregon Chai

Heather, Brian, Lori and Tedde, 1996

Street scene in India, 1998

Brewing chai in a concession in India, 1998

Brewing chai outside a monument in New Delhi, India, 1998

Nirvana in a Cup: The founding of Oregon Chai

Harvesting sugar cane in India, 1998

Tea plantation in India, 1998

Women tea pickers carrying tea leaves to processing plant, 1998

Tedde at the Terai Indian Planters' Association in India, 1998

SECTION V:

Reading The Tea Leaves

The Beginning of the End

During the holidays I vacationed for a week. I shopped. I visited the zoo and readied myself for Christmas celebrations with family. After the New Year's celebration, consisting of me lounging blithely on the couch while my husband lit fireworks in our driveway, I returned to work refreshed and re-energized.

The first thing I did was examine all of my open invoices. When I finished reconciling our inventory, I was so elated that I hop-skipped down the hall to our accountant's office. I entered, beaming and began discussing my file with him.

"I was just going through these invoices --"

"You don't do that anymore," he said, interrupting me.

His abruptness surprised me. I was shocked.

"What?" I asked. "What do you mean: 'I don't do that anymore?'"

He put down the book he was holding and looked directly at me.

"You don't handle the purchasing or invoices anymore," he said. "The Production Manager handles them now."

"What? No, I handle them," I insisted.

I leafed through the file I held in my shaking hand, peering at the names of our vendors. I was confused. "Who says I don't?" I asked finally. "No one told me!"

We stood there facing one another for what seemed like hours, but in reality it was just a few long minutes.

A stand off.

He tried to take the file from my hand. I stared in amazement. I clung to it and in a childlike tug-of-war, we yanked the file back and forth. I couldn't believe it. We were acting like a couple of preschoolers. Finally, hesitantly, I just let go. It was becoming all too clear.

"I want to talk to the production manager," I said and called my assistant into the office.

"Who authorized this change?" I asked.

"I met with the Chairman of the Board over the holidays and we decided it would be best if I handled all the purchasing and invoicing," he said flatly. "It's now my responsibility."

My ears stung. I could barely breathe. What is he talking about?

What was he doing meeting with the Chairman of the Board over the holidays? Behind my back?! What was this "we decided?" Who the hell was he? My assistant? To go over my head and tell me what he and the Chairman of the Board had decided? I was livid. I realized right in that moment how much of my identity had been wrapped up in my position, in my company. This was my life. And it had been for the past several years. He was dismantling my career out from underneath me, one task at a time.

I felt as if my heart had stopped. I was embarrassed, hurt and disappointed. My face burned, humiliated. My shoulders sagged. I turned, unable to think of a single appropriate thing to say while suppressing the string of inappropriate things that I had to hold back with contempt from spilling from my mouth. I trudged, fuming, out of the room.

When I returned to my office, I collapsed in my chair. What happened while I was away? I was only gone a week. Over the holidays! Don't these people ever take a break? It gnawed at my stomach. I called Heather.

"Did you know about these changes?" I asked.

Her voice sounded tense. "Mom, it only makes sense," she said.

My stomach dropped. My heart broke. She knew.

"He needs to take full responsibility for all parts of production," she tried to explain.

I was floored. How was it that everybody knew about this except for me? How could this happen? How could someone take away my work? He was stealing my job. I adored my position. Everyone - including our Board's chair - was always telling me what an excellent job I did. How could they do this to me?

Nirvana in a Cup: The founding of Oregon Chai

I saw a tear drop onto my desk. My worst fears had come true: I was no longer needed at Oregon Chai. At least not in any capacity that interested me.

For several weeks afterward, I numbly re-played the conversation I'd had with our accountant over and over again in my head. I still could not believe my responsibilities had been handed over to my assistant, to someone that had been there less than a year and, in my opinion, was still learning the ropes. I assumed everyone else must think he could do a better job than me. He was, after all, an experienced, industry professional and I was what? A "housewife" who was just lucky to have stumbled across a great recipe with world class timing?

Oregon Chai now employed over twenty people, including sales representatives working from their homes in various parts of the country. With our increased staff and warehouse needs, we needed a new home. My husband, the architect, was charged with finding us new quarters.

After examining several properties, he finally found one that would work: a large, cave-like space formerly used as a photographer's studio. We hired him to remodel it so that it would accommodate our needs. Following its metamorphosis, it housed numerous cozy offices and a lab. Reflecting our product's appeal, it featured Oregon Chai colors both inside and out. It was the ideal business home.

To celebrate our open house in the new building, we hired Maggie to develop recipes using Oregon Chai's own products - and she did not disappoint. She generated all sorts of terrific ideas and even catered one of our Christmas parties - making everything from chicken satay and pâté to bread and cookies - all using the various flavors of Oregon Chai.

After nearly a year of trying to fit in to my new, reduced and less satisfying role, I decided the best thing I could do for myself, both physically and mentally, was to resign.

I composed myself.

I went in to Heather's office.

And I quit.

"But, Mom, I want you here," I heard my daughter say. "Won't you continue on as a consultant?"

"I'd rather not," I answered flatly, trying hard to keep my emotions in check. I was sure this was what was best for me. Well, pretty sure.

"But both our Board's chair and I feel you've done a good job developing new products in the past," she insisted. "We want you to continue to oversee research and development."

"I don't want to develop new products or oversee research and development. I'm not the right person for that job, I'm sorry honey, I just don't think I can do it anymore. I'm sorry, but it's time." I said, not wanting to lose it with her, not wanting her to see me cry and not wanting to hurt her feelings. I knew this was just how it was, I knew it was coming.

Leaving Oregon Chai was one of the most difficult decisions I've ever made in my entire life. For almost a decade, Oregon Chai was my identity and I tried desperately to hang on. But I realized I had to let go.

For several months following my departure, I visited a counselor to help with this difficult transition. I couldn't believe that I could go from a strong confident woman just a few years earlier to feeling like I was about to have a nervous breakdown.

It helped me to think about great men, like our second president, John Adams, who experienced conflicting feelings when he left his office. I recall reading one particular passage in David McCullough's, *John Adams* that gave me comfort:

"Alive and hearty he was and remarkably so, all things considered. He was a picture of health as visitors and family members would attest. He still nursed wounds of defeat; he could brood over past insults; he longed for vindication and for gratitude for so much that he had done and the sacrifices he had made...Yet...he claimed to be happier than he had ever been, which if said partly for effect - as a matter of pride - was also fundamentally true, once the initial years of retirement had passed and particularly after he began writing again."

This inspired me to start writing my own memoirs more as journal therapy than ever really thinking it would actually be published. Parts of it were enjoyable as I reminisced about the wonderful experiences I had had at Oregon Chai - but not every memory was a good one. Obviously. Some proved so painful that I couldn't face the page for days - but somehow, I worked through all that to get it down.

It would have been unfair and unreasonable for me to leave immediately. I stayed long enough to ease the transition. Awkward and uncomfortable as it was, I knew increasingly that I had made the right decision and began to feel lighter, liberated. It was going to be okay.

I remained a consultant mainly to support Heather if she needed it, but the sands of time were shifting beneath all of us. It was hard for any of us to know where we stood - or what our roles were as they seemed to change so fast.

Lori hired an assistant and with the help of consultants, still ruled our marketing department. It was a couple of years before they hired a marketing vice president responsible for directing her department.

Heather's departure from Oregon Chai was much more gradual, beginning with the birth of her first child. After having two miscarriages, she was eager to focus on the health and happiness of her baby and slow down professionally.

She was still the company's President and C.E.O. and still the driving force motivating the sales team and Oregon Chai's lead spokesperson appearing on national television, but there was light at the end of her tunnel as well. She was ready to get off this train, too.

CHAPTER 27

Going Out with a Bang!

In 2002, Heather and I were scheduled for an appearance on "Food Nation," a half-hour program featured on the Food Network. Prior to the show, its producer requested that we perform a public chai-making demonstration.

Heather and I fretted over this for several days. Obviously, we couldn't hand over our Oregon Chai recipe to the public yet our goal was to create a delicious beverage, one that audience members would enjoy and could reproduce at home.

I worked on several different recipes and finally opted for one that both Heather and I thought was presentable. It certainly wasn't Oregon Chai Original, but it offered an acceptable flavor. And since Heather wished to use the Oregon Chai brand on the show, we opted to blend it into a chai milkshake. We both felt it was the ideal strategy.

On the day of the show I was all nerves. I'd been on stage and appeared before cameras before, but this time was different. I wanted the chai to taste good. I wanted the host, Bobby Flay, to profess "Mmm, this is delicious!" We'd altered our production process a bit for easier filming, so I kept tasting the chai throughout the show, making certain it was all right.

When it came time to blend the milkshake, we encountered a problem. We were midway through taping and needed the ice cream, which Heather had placed in the microwave to soften a bit. But we'd let it heat too long. It was mush and we didn't have more. It was too saucy for a milkshake, but we had no choice. We blended it anyhow. Fortunately, the resulting beverage tasted so good that Bobby Flay grinned in pure pleasure, praising us on camera.

I got what I wanted.

"This is good!" he kept saying. "Isn't this good?"

When the show aired I was disappointed to see that due to my anxiety over the chai we were brewing, I appeared to be chewing on my lip. Ugh, I thought, why did I do that? I simply was not aware of it at the time. However, Heather came across smiling and friendly and Bobby Flay liked our product so it was worth it.

Over the next couple of years, the program re-aired several more times and each time, there I was, still nervously chewing on my lip. Nonetheless, the exposure proved to be invaluable for our brand. Though it was our customers who loved the taste, it was the press that helped spread the word about our delicious, retro tonic. We couldn't have been luckier.

Carla resigned a couple of years after me. She had wanted to retire for sometime. Her husband was retired and they were looking forward to traveling and playing lots of golf.

In 2004, Oregon Chai was sold to Kerry Foods for seventy-five million dollars.

I could hardly believe it. What had started as Heather's simple idea of a delicious, traditional Indian beverage resulted in endless memories and ultimately made everyone rich. All of our founders, consultants and investors who had placed so much of their faith in our precarious start-up received substantial returns on their investment.

We had had countless good times along with a few rough times. We disagreed, sometimes strongly, but always remained friends. We followed the path before us, which opened its doors to places and people we could never have imagined. We were fortunate. Not all stories have such happy endings.

Was it karma that compelled Oregon Chai, the all-natural, best-tasting chai in the world, to emerge as one of the best experiences of my life? I don't know, but I remain thankful, blessed that I was given a role to play in our amazing adventure. It was a great ride.

Oregon Chai corporate headquarters remodeled by architect David McMillen. Portland, Oregon, 1999

BUSINESS SHAPING THE WEST

The Chai's the limit

by Harry Carpenter

HEATHER HOWITT IS ALL ABOUT CHAI. She began drinking the spicy herbal concoctions in college, found them even more tantalizing during her travels to India and China, obsessed over them in Boulder, Colorado, then turned her obsession into passion and a full-time occupation in her beloved city of Portland, Oregon.

Heather and her mother, Tedde McMillen, founded Oregon Chai together in April 1994. "If my mom hadn't applied for the business license, Oregon Chai may have never been," says Heather. But Tedde did. And in October of 1994 the company was incorporated officially.

Since 1996 the mother-daughter combination have enjoyed 300% annual growth, and were named the third fastest growing company the past two years running by the Portland Business Journal. "My mom perfected the recipes and I sold them to the stores. That's the way it all began." Presently, Oregon Chai employs 19 people in a newly refurbished 9,000-square-foot warehouse space near the Pearl district in Portland, Oregon.

When asked her secret for success, two words surface continually: Passion and quality. "Stick it out," Heather recommends. "If you are passionate about what you are doing, that passion will carry you through the difficult times."

As for quality she says, "We don't strive to make a healthy drink, we strive to make a quality drink." Indeed, it is quality that permeates everything Heather Howitt does. She leads an extremely active lifestyle, making time for long runs and hikes through Forest Park and the greater Portland area. She manages a multimillion-dollar corporation while also raising a seven-week-old baby boy.

Heather believes in hiring good people who share her passion—for chai and for life. She espouses a flexible management style that rewards employees for jobs well done. The corporate climate is loose and fun, with emphasis on the bottom line. "We work hard," Heather asserts, "But we believe in having fun while we're doing it."

To illustrate the point, Oregon Chai has a climbing wall on-site and Heather insists on off-site meetings to get employees out in the fresh air, freeing up their minds and their thinking. She once held a corporate review at a cabin atop a local mountain. "Some people thought it corny," she reflects. "And I was exhausted after the long hike, as I'm sure many others were, but the take-away was organic and ex-

Heather Howitt

is **proof positive**

that you can

have it all.

SKYWEST MAGAZINE • WINTER 2000

32

Article in Skywest Magazine, 2000

Epilogue

After the sale to Kerry Group a close friend asked, "What did that mean to you?"

"What?" I said. "The sale of Oregon Chai to Kerry Group: what did it mean to me personally?"

"Yeah, did it change you? You know, how did you feel? Did it change the way you live? I mean, come on, you're rich and successful. Didn't that make a difference? Aren't you thrilled? Everybody wants to win the lottery. You did. Tell me what it's like."

"So you're asking; did the sale change my life? Well, not really. Yes, I now have more money in the bank but I'm still a pretty frugal person. You're right, I am better off and it did free me up so that I don't have to worry, at least for a few years. At least, for now, I don't need to be extra careful about money and watch my budget. I mean, if I wanted to do something, I pretty much could."

My friend really caught me off guard. I didn't know how I felt. I just never thought about it. I hated to say it meant nothing. The money was great but I'm not an extravagant person. I don't buy fancy clothes. I wouldn't buy a thousand dollar purse or a five-hundred dollar blouse or shoes. That's just not me. Even though I might be able to now, I just wouldn't feel good about it.

My values haven't changed. I feel like I always have: there are so many people in this world that are needy that it doesn't seem right for me to live so lavishly. For me, it has always been important to make a contribution.

I told my friend: "When the Kerry Group purchased Oregon Chai, what excited me most, I think, was the fact that everybody who had been willing and able to help us out, to get the project off the ground, family members who had loaned us money and taken stock as repayment, our first investor who had faith in us, our consultants who saw our potential, and even the employees who were given stock and options - everyone finally got rewarded.

That made me feel great. It was a nice return for people who worked hard, who had put their trust in Heather and me. It made me feel good that they weren't disappointed. I mean, in the past, I'd invested money in the stock market only to see it, as we did in 2000, slowly, or sometimes quickly, slip away.

I think that's what was most important to me, more important than anything else. The fact that everybody, everybody, who was so supportive, and maybe people who just thought, you know: "Hey, this might be a hot investment," realized a substantial gain. I mean, it really paid off! Yeah, that's what it meant to me."

I guess from the moment it was first suggested that the company might sell, I was a little complacent. From just about the first year, people and companies asked, "Are you interested in selling?" We'd get excited, and then we would either decide we just weren't ready or the parties would lose interest.

This happened so often, I finally got to a point that it was kind of like the little boy who cried wolf, I just wrote them off and didn't pay much attention. I think the difference in this particular sale was that the Board initiated the transaction. They hired an investment banker to see if there was a market for the company. That was their goal from Day One: to get in and get out - with a profit. That's what they do.

We were fortunate. Oregon Chai, Inc. got a very good deal from a wonderful company who shared a lot of our same values: sustainable business practices; supporting the environment; being socially responsible by buying fair traded products; and by using organic ingredients that they purchase from a company that grows spices in and in such a way as to protect and preserve the rain forests. These things were much more important to me.

What the sale also did for me was broaden my choices. Now I don't have to take a job that I might not enjoy. I could help those in need, like my family. You know, I guess I was kind of a socialist at heart. I'd always felt the world would be a better place if more people had opportunities, housing and jobs they enjoyed.

My father spent most of his life in positions that he hated and he would often complain. He was a miserable man and I swore I would never live like that and I've been very fortunate because of Oregon Chai. I didn't have to do that, to accept a position out of need. Wouldn't it be wonderful if everybody had those choices? The sale gave me choices about how I could spend my time, the opportunity to do as I wished. And, as I said, I felt it was really important to make a contribution, to use the knowledge I'd gained in some meaningful way. I started mentoring others who wanted to bring food products to market.

Oh yeah, the money was great. Don't get me wrong there. After the sale we installed an irrigation system - which was a godsend after more than twenty years of dragging soaker hoses and sprinklers all over the yard and we added a sunroom to the side of our house. But, you know, when you're sixty years old and you've been frugal all your life and you've been very careful, it's hard to change.

After the sale I no longer had to use coupons at the grocery store. When we were first married, my husband was in college and I had to be very careful with the little money we had. I remember one time I bought a package of eight frankfurters. I figured that gave us enough for two meals. The first night we each ate two hot dogs. After consuming his, my husband went to the refrigerator to get a third one and I said, "If you eat that tonight, you will only have one tomorrow." He went without. But today he could have that third. However, now we have other limitations. We both have to watch our weight, our cholesterol and blood sugar. But the sale to Kerry Group made it possible for me to go to the store and buy beautiful organic food and produce or whatever I want, even though it may cost a bit more and yes, my husband can have that extra hot-dog, if he wants.

Finally, the most important fact for me was that I made a contribution. Success for me wasn't about the amount of money I made but about the sense of accomplishment. I felt good. I started a great little business. I took pride in a product that not only tasted good, but became the leader of the category. I loved my work. I saw my daughter succeed - isn't that a mother's best wish come true to see her child blossom? And, I have been able to help others. That's how I measure success.

Recipes

Refreshingly Simple

COLD DRINKS

Citrus Spritzer, Apple Spritzer, Berrichai Spritzer,
Lemonade Spritzer, Orchard Spritzer, Cream Sodas,
Banana Chai Smoothie, Cantaloupe Frappé, Chai Chiller™,
Chai Shake, ChaiScream™ Cooler

MIXED DRINKS

Chai-Tai, Himalayan Sunrise, Black Afghan, White Chai Russian,
Long Island Iced Chai, Frozen Banana Chai Daiquiri

Citrus Spritzer*

- 4 oz. Original Chai concentrate
- 4 oz. sparkling water
- 1-1/2 tsp. lemon or 2 tsp. orange syrup

Combine the above ingredients over ice.
Add a twist of lemon or orange.

Apple Spritzer*

- 4 oz. Original Chai concentrate
- 4 oz. sparkling water
- 4 tsp. apple syrup

Combine the above ingredients.
Serve cold, over ice.

Berrichai Spritzer*

- 4 oz. Original Chai concentrate
- 4 oz. sparkling water
- 2 tsp. blackberry, raspberry or blueberry syrup
- 2 oz. cream or half & half (optional)

Combine the above ingredients over ice.
Add a twist of lemon, orange or skewer of berries.

Orchard Spritzer*

- 4 oz. Original Chai concentrate
- 2 oz. sparkling water
- 4 oz. apple (or pear) cider or juice

Mix the above ingredients together. Serve cold, over ice.

* Recipe created by Polly Wood of Polly's Cakes.

LEMONADE SPRITZER

- 4 oz. Original Chai concentrate
- 4 oz. lemonade
- 2 oz. sparking water

Combine the above ingredients.
Stir and serve with a lemon twist or fruit skewer.

CREAM SODAS*

- 4 oz. Oregon Chai concentrate *(Original, Caffeine Free, Kashmir Green Tea, or Slightly Sweet)*
- 2 oz. sparkling water
- 2 oz. cream or half & half

Combine the above ingredients over ice.

BANANA CHAI SMOOTHIE*

- 4 oz. Original Chai concentrate
- 4 oz. water
- 1 medium banana (4 oz. peeled)
- 2 oz. crushed ice (2 cubes)

Puree Original Chai concentrate, water, banana and ice
cubes in blender. Serve immediately.

CANTALOUPE FRAPPÉ*

- 4 oz. Original Chai concentrate
- 4 oz. fresh cantaloupe, cubed
- 2 oz. crushed ice (2 cubes)
- 1 oz. fresh or frozen blueberries (optional)

Place Original Chai concentrate, cantaloupe and ice
in blender and puree. Serve immediately.

---

* Recipe created by Polly Wood of Polly's Cakes.

CHAI CHILLER™

- 8 oz. ice
- 6 oz. Oregon Chai concentrate *(Original, Caffeine Free, Kashmir Green Tea, or Slightly Sweet)*
- 2 oz. powdered, non-dairy creamer
- Whipping cream
- Toppings: candied sprinkles, chopped nuts

In a blender combine ice, chai concentrate and non-dairy creamer. Blend until smooth. To serve, top with whipping cream and decorate with sprinkles or nuts.

CHAI SHAKE

- Ice Cream
- Oregon Chai concentrate *(Original, Caffeine Free, Kashmir Green Tea, or Slightly Sweet)*

Using your favorite milkshake recipe, add chai concentrate in place of milk.

CHAISCREAM COOLER™

- 4 oz. crushed ice
- 4 oz. whole milk
- 4 oz. Oregon Chai concentrate *(Original, Caffeine Free, Kashmir Green Tea, or Slightly Sweet)*
- 4 oz. ice cream
- Whipping cream

In blender combine ice, milk, chai concentrate and ice cream. Blend until smooth.

CHAI-TAI*

- 2 oz. rum
- 2 oz. Original Chai concentrate
- 1 Tbsp. lemon juice
- 1 oz. triple sec
- 1 Tbsp. grenadine
- Orange slice

Blend rum, Original Chai concentrate, lemon juice and triple sec
in a shaker over ice. Strain into a tall glass and add
grenadine and a slice of orange.

HIMALAYAN SUNRISE*

- 2 oz. tequila
- 2 oz. Original Chai concentrate
- 4 oz. orange juice
- 1 Tbsp. grenadine

Mix first thee ingredients over ice. Strain into a highball glass.
Add ice cubes. Pour in grenadine slowly and allow to settle.
Stir before drinking.

BLACK AFGHAN*

- 2 oz. Original Chai concentrate
- 1 oz. water
- 1 oz. amaretto
- 1 oz. vodka

Combine above ingredients and pour over ice.

---

* Recipe created by Polly Wood of Polly's Cakes.

WHITE CHAI RUSSIAN*

- 2 oz. Original Chai concentrate
- 1 oz. cream
- 1 oz. amaretto
- 1 oz. vodka
- 1/2 & 1/2 to taste

Combine above ingredients and pour over ice.

LONG ISLAND ICED CHAI*

- 2 oz. Original Chai concentrate
- 1/2 oz. rum
- 1/2 oz. vodka
- 1/2 oz. triple sec
- 1/2 oz. gin
- 1/2 oz. lemon juice
- 3 oz. orange juice

Mix above ingredients in a highball glass over ice. Garnish with a slice of lemon or orange or a sprig of mint.

FROZEN BANANA CHAI DAIQUIRI*

- 1-1/2 oz. Original Chai concentrate
- 1-1/2 oz. rum
- 1 medium banana, sliced
- 1 cup crushed ice

Combine above ingredients in a blender and blend at low speed
for 5 seconds then blend at high speed until firm.
Pour into champagne glasses, top with a banana slice

* Recipe created by Polly Wood of Polly's Cakes.

Let's Eat

SAUCES
Original Chai Marinade

VEGETABLES
Chai Candied Yams

DESSERTS
Pear Frangipane Tart, Poached Pear Halves,
Chocolate Chai Roulade, Strawberry Pie

SNACKS
Spiced Chai Pecans, Spicy Cocoa-Chai Pecans

ORIGINAL CHAI MARINADE*

- 1 cup Original concentrate
- 1/4 cup canola oil
- 1/2 tsp. cardamom
- 2 Tbsp. shallot, minced
- 1 clove garlic, minced
- 1 tsp. fresh ginger, minced
- 2 Tbsp. tamari
- 2 Tbsp. sundried tomato paste

Combine above ingredients. Marinate chicken, flank steak, mahi-mahi, eggplant, shitake or portabella mushrooms and grill.

CHAI CANDIED YAMS

- 4 small yams, peeled & quartered
- Original chai concentrate
- 2 Tbsp. butter
- 1/3 cup maple syrup
- 1/4 cup chicken broth

Place yams in pan. Cover with cold water and 1/2 cup chai concentrate. Bring to a boil. Reduce heat; simmer until tender but still firm, about 20 minutes. Drain well. Melt butter in a skillet.
Add maple syrup and 1/3 cup chai concentrate. Simmer over low heat until slightly reduced, about 15 minutes. Add yams and stir until lightly coated. Add chicken broth and simmer over low heat 10 more minutes. Serve immediately.

* Recipe created by Polly Wood of Polly's Cakes.

POACHED PEAR HALVES*

- 2 quarts Original concentrate
- 5 ripe pears

Pour Oregon Chai concentrate into a 4-quart pan. Peel, halve and core pears and add immediately to pan. Cover with a round of parchment that has a hole in the center. Bring to boil over medium heat and remove from stove. Cool in liquid and refrigerate pears in the chai syrup.

If any syrup is left over, reduce it by 1/2 and it makes a great glaze. You may also save the syrup for poaching pears another time.

* Recipe created by Polly Wood of Polly's Cakes.

PEAR FRANGIPANE*

- 1 unbaked 10" pastry shell
- 8 oz. almond paste
- 4 oz. brown sugar
- 5 oz. white sugar
- 4 large eggs
- 1/2 lb. butter, softened
- Grated zest of 1 orange or 1 tsp. dried
- 1/2 tsp. ground cardamom
- 1 tsp. vanilla
- 2-1/2 oz. flour
- 1/2 tsp. baking powder
- 10 Oregon Chai Poached Pear Halves**

Frangipane:

Blend almond paste, sugars and 1 egg in mixer. Beat with paddle attachment on medium speed until smooth. Add butter, spices and vanilla. Beat in the remaining eggs, one at a time. Combine flour and baking powder. Slow mixer to first setting; add flour mixture until just absorbed. Makes enough filling for three 10" tarts. Frangipane freezes well for 1 month.

Assembly:

Spread 1/3 of the frangipane evenly on the bottom of the tart shell. Set each pear half, cut side down, and cut crosswise into thin slices. Use a metal spatula to move each sliced pear onto the frangipane. Arrange pear halves around the edge of the tart and one pear half in the middle.

Bake at 350 degrees F for 45 minutes or until frangipane is set. Cool. Brush with pear-chai syrup from poached pears.

* Recipe created by Polly Wood of Polly's Cakes.

** See Poached Pears Halves on previous page.

CHOCOLATE CHAI ROULADE

Filling: (prepare in advance)
- 6 oz semi-sweet chocolate chips
- 1 teaspoon Oregon Chai Tea Latte Mix
- 2 oz butter
- 3/4 cups heavy cream

Cake:
- 3 1/2 oz unsweetened chocolate
- 3⁄4 oz butter
- 2 teaspoons Oregon Chai Tea Latte Mix
- 1/16 teaspoon salt
- 1/2 cup walnuts chopped
- 1/4 cup Oregon Chai Slightly Sweet Chai concentrate
- 4 large eggs, separated (discard one egg-yolk)
- 3 Tablespoons sugar

Filling:
Combine chocolate and butter in the top of a double-boiler pan and melt over simmering water, stirring occasionally. Remove from heat and stir in Oregon Chai Tea Latte Mix. Remove pan from hot water and slowly beat in cream until smooth. Cover and refrigerate until cooled.

Cake:
Preheat over to 350 degree Fahrenheit. Grease 11 1⁄2 by 16 1⁄2 inch sheet and line with parchment or waxed paper, leaving extra inches on ends.

Combine chocolate, Oregon Chai Slightly Sweet Chai concentrate and butter in the top of a double-boiler pan and melt over simmering water, stirring occasionally. Add Oregon Chai Tea Latte Mix and stir until smooth. Beat in 3 egg yolks, one at a time.

Combine 4 egg whites and salt in a large bowl and beat until soft peaks form. Slowly add sugar, beating until the whites hold soft peaks. Fold about 1 cup of egg whites into chocolate mixture, then gently fold the whites into the batter. Scrape batter into pan and bake in the middle of the oven until the cake is firm to touch, about 15 minutes.

Remove pan from oven. Cover with a lightly dampened tea towel and let cool, about 20 minutes. When cool, cover with a cookie sheet or jelly roll pan and invert. Peel off parchment, replace with a clean piece of paper and another pan and invert again.

Position cake horizontally, spread all but about 3⁄4 cup of the filling evenly over the cake. Starting with the long edge closest to you, roll up the cake. Place the roulade seam side down on a cookie sheet. Trim the edges and spread the remaining icing over the cake. Sprinkle with chopped walnuts. Cut into 1-inch slices, Serves 8.

Will keep 5 days under refrigeration.

Based on a recipe for Mexican Chocolate Roulade by Joanna Pruess, "Specialty Food Magazine", June 2003, page 36.

STRAWBERRY PIE

- 1 pre-cooked pastry shell, cooled
- 1-2 quarts fresh ORGANIC strawberries
- 1/2 cup strawberries, crushed
- 1/2 cup ORIGINAL, ORGANIC or CAFFEINE FREE Oregon Chai concentrate
- 2 Tablespoons. sugar
- 2 teaspoons cornstarch
- Red Food Coloring
- Whipping Cream

Clean strawberries, crush or puree 1/2 cup and set aside. Cut and arrange the remaining berries in piecrust. Set aside.

Make glaze: combine crushed berries and Oregon Chai concentrate in saucepan. Bring to boil, reduce heat to medium and cook 2-3 minutes, stirring frequently. In a separate bowl, combine sugar and cornstarch and mix well. Strain cooked juice into sugar mixture and mix well.

Return sugar/juice mixture to saucepan. Cook until clear and thickened, stirring constantly. Remove from heat, add food coloring to desired color. Cool slightly. Spoon over strawberries in pie shell.

Serve immediately. Top with whipped cream, if desired.

SPICED CHAI PECANS

- 1 cup whole pecans
- 1 egg white
- 2 Tablespoons water
- 1/8th teaspoon salt
- 1 package - 0.8oz. Oregon Chai SPICED Original Tea Latte Mix

Preheat over to 225° F.

Combine the salt and Oregon Chai SPICED Original Tea
Latte Mix in a large bowl. Set aside.

In a separate bowl, beat the egg whites and water until frothy. Add pecans, turning
several times to coat with the egg whites. Transfer the nuts to a strainer and let them
stand for a couple of minutes to let any excess egg white drip off.

Transfer the nuts to the spice mixture, turning to coat all pecans evenly.

Spread nuts evenly on a sheet so they are not touching. Bake for 15 minutes; using a
spatula, loosen and turn them. Continue doing this every 15 minutes until the nuts
are crisp and dry, about 1 hour, 15 minutes total time.

Remove from oven and cool. Place in a covered container. Will keep 3 days at room
temperature; 3 weeks in cool storage.

From a recipe for Spicy Cocoa Pecans, by Joanna Pruess, "Specialty Food Magazine", June 2003, page 34.

Spicy Cocoa-Chai Pecans

- 1 cup whole pecans
- 1 egg white
- 2 Tablespoons water
- 2 Tablespoons fine sugar
- 1/8th teaspoon salt
- 1/8th teaspoon cocoa powder
- 1/8th teaspoon chili powder
- 1/4 teaspoon Oregon Chai Tea Latte Mix (or 1⁄4 teaspoon ground cinnamon)
- dash cayenne pepper, optional

Preheat over to 225° F.

Combine sugar, salt, cocoa powder, chili powder,
Oregon Chai Tea Latte Mix in a large bowl. Set aside.

In a separate bowl, beat the egg whites and water until frothy.
Add pecans, turning several times to coat with the egg whites. Transfer the nuts to
a strainer and let them stand for a couple of minutes to let any excess egg white drip
off.

Transfer the nuts to the spice mixture, turning to coat all pecans evenly.

Spread nuts evenly on a sheet so they are not touching.
Bake for 15 minutes; using a spatula, loosen and turn them.
Continue doing this every 15 minutes until the nuts are crisp and dry, about 1 hour,
15 minutes total time.
Remove from oven and cool. Place in a covered container. Will keep 3 days at room
temperature; 3 weeks in cool storage.

From a recipe for Spicy Cocoa Pecans, by Joanna Pruess, "Specialty Food Magazine", June 2003, page 34.